WHERE WILL YOUR NEXT STEPS TAKE YOU?

A guide
to discovering yourself
and finding a career that fits

DIANE SINGER

Publisher's Information

EBookBakery Books

Author contact: dsinger962@gmail.com

ISBN 978-1-938517-85-3

© 2019 by Diane Singer

Disclaimer: This book is intended to be a guide. It is not intended as a replacement or as a substitute for a psychologist, social worker or professional counselor. The business information is not a substitute for the advice of an accountant or an attorney. The author disclaims any liability from the use of information in this book.

DEDICATION

Dedicated to my late husband, Stanley Berger,
a very good person, a loving husband
and a wonderful father who inspired his children and me
to always do the right thing and be the best that we can be.
If everyone even had some of his qualities,
the world would be a better place.

Dedicated to my late brother, Marvin Bloom.
He won the Science Fair Award at the Cotting School for Special Needs Students.
He passed away at an early age from Muscular Dystrophy.
This book was written in honor of him.
He never had the opportunity to live up to his potential.

ACKNOWLEDGMENTS

My sincere thanks and gratitude to my husband, Sam, for his encouragement and support throughout this journey.

This workbook might not have been a reality without the support of my daughters, Melissa and Nanci, and their beautiful families who make me so proud.

EXECUTIVE SUMMARY

Combining positive psychology with proven job search skills and techniques, *Where Will Your Next Steps Take You?* helps people deal with obstacles on their way to success. Then readers follow a step-by-step process to understand what is important in a career, assess their skills and talents, and conduct a well planned job search campaign.

The Audience:

The book is designed for both motivated individuals and as a guide for counselors, coaches, mentors and community organizations that work with potential job seekers in a one-to-one setting or in group workshops.

The Need:

Everyone wants to get ahead, but life does not come without challenges. Difficult times require effective strategies to manage your career. To get a head start, you need to utilize different methods. The guide combines Cognitive Behavior Therapy (CBT) with career development. CBT is based on proven behavioral research directed toward solving current problems and thus change how you look at a situation. Many studies have shown that CBT is an effective way to manage goal-oriented change.

The Methodology:

In the first part of the book, Issues and Strategies, you'll learn coping skills to manage emotions and deal with anxiety so you cope better with life's challenges. These skills will build lasting change. You will gain a better understanding of ways to manage problems. Overall, you will develop a stronger sense of well-being.

In the second part, Career Search Tools and Resources, you will develop an effective plan for finding a career. Finding a good match between your needs and your career that gives you satisfaction is a process that takes advantage of your capabilities. Your existing skills and experience might be used with some modifications or with additional training and education, depending on the chosen career.

You will be guided through the worksheets to recognize your strengths. Then apply the user-friendly tools and resources to move forward.

The Call To Action:

The benefits continue long after going through the exercises in this book. You will understand what you really want in a career, and how to integrate it with your personal life. Each worksheet becomes part of the decision-making process: your choices, your characteristics and your future. The book presents the nuts and bolts of a career search: decision-making tools, training and education, job search strategies and more. All the information and resources are designed to help you succeed in conducting a well-designed job search, expand your horizons or even change careers. It will help position you for success in today's challenging environment.

CONTENTS

PART I: ISSUES AND STRATEGIES

Heighten your awareness of the issues that you deal with. This is the first step to understanding what has made life more difficult and how to live a more meaningful life.

Recognize what your triggers are. Use coping skills to deal with difficult situations. Acknowledge your thoughts and feelings. Learn to respond in more positive ways.

Learn strategies to manage stress. It's about learning how happiness and gratitude can help in all parts of your life.

You will see the benefits of moving forward. Have a mentor on your side to help you see the possibilities ahead.

Take a situation and turn it into an opportunity. You will learn better habits to set and reach goals. Give yourself more credit for what you accomplish.

Clarify what you want. The process of change includes ways to make better choices based on good information and realistic expectations.

PART II: CAREER SEARCH TOOLS AND RESOURCES

Chapter 7 is packed with information to help you match your strengths with your values and identify what you want in a career. Many resources are included to help locate job training organizations.

Be aware of roadblocks you might encounter. As you evaluate different options to handle problems, you will become more flexible and see the world as one with more opportunities.

Learn about networking, job fairs, job leads, application forms, resumes and interviewing skills. Understand how to present yourself to your best advantage.

Obtain information to develop a business plan. Learn how to create a need, market your business, locate financing and attend workshops to help the small business owner.

Resources are included for those who have transitioned from the military to civilian life on where to find housing, medical care, employment and additional support services.

The strategies in this book are important but the overall goal is to use them and keep going forward. As you practice resilience and optimism skills, you will begin to see the benefits and create a better life for you and your family.

INTRODUCTION

Where Will Your Next Steps Take You? takes stock of your personal and work experiences to reveal an accurate assessment of where you are now. This paves the way for the direction you want to go. **Part One, Issues and Strategies,** teaches coping skills to deal with life's challenges. P**art Two, Career Search Tools and Resources,** provides detailed information on career training, education, and being a great candidate for the career you choose.

Part One: Issues And Strategies

The core of the book demonstrates how awareness, coping skills, mindfulness and tension-reducing tools successfully deal with obstacles that could get in the way of getting ahead. The section on values helps you to clarify what is important to you and your family. Because most people can benefit from speaking to someone such as a mentor, there is also a chapter on ways to find one and on how he or she can help.

Part Two: Career Search Tools And Resources

This section contains detailed information on what you need to know to make a career move. The principles and resources will guide you. Choose goals that motivate you and help you make a better decision. You will learn strategies and gain the knowledge you need to be better prepared. There are many resources on training, education, scholarships and more to help you succeed. A section for veterans gives many resources for support services. Another section provides guidance for those considering self-employment.

This book is not only about how to get a better job. It is also about learning about yourself and feeling empowered about what you can do. By going through these chapters you will have a practical tool for mapping out a realistic path for where you want to be.

Many things in life are unpredictable but the next part of your life does not have to be.

1

CHANGE STARTS HERE

HAVE YOU BEEN TRYING for a better life and are not where you want to be yet? To get a good start, you need to make a plan. Move forward and find a new direction.

WHAT DID YOU WANT TO BE?

Do you remember being asked, "What do you want to be when you grow up?" Many of us did not know that there were so many choices. Now that you are older, ask yourself: Do you have a strong desire or yen to be _____?

As adults, we might realize how strongly we were influenced by our family or the neighborhood we grew up in. What if you didn't have a strong role model? If life was tough, that spark probably went dim as you needed to survive. You might have forgotten those dreams that you had when you were young. When we are in survival mode, we think of status quo, not necessarily about how to get ahead.

By connecting to your talents and abilities, you can launch yourself and show others how to find their way too. Everyone has something to offer. It is important to treat yourself with care so you can give yourself a chance. Don't mistake opinions for truth. Hope is a start, but to make changes, you need a plan based on realistic expectations in order to succeed. A better life means different things to different people: a steady income, finding work you enjoy doing, supporting your family, and believing in yourself. The reality is that when we pay attention and listen to our inner voices, we become more aware of who we are and what life can be.

Awareness:

Awareness is sensing your emotions and behaviors. It is important to put a situation in perspective. Put your head around it. Tell yourself, "I am worth it." Be understanding and give yourself credit for starting. Remind yourself that the decisions you made before do not define who you are now. To grow, it is essential to increase your awareness and willingness to admit, even to yourself, what might be holding you back. Facing these issues is not easy. You will learn different ways to view a situation. Life is a process and growth is possible, even with some struggles. Your willingness to address what is important will keep you moving forward.

Understanding Yourself:

It is common for people to resist the self-assessment process even if it's done alone. If you feel that way, be kind to yourself. Give yourself credit for starting. Recognize that your feelings are normal. Every so often, give yourself a break. Remind yourself that the decisions you made in the past do not define who you are now. Your good qualities will give you strength when you learn to trust yourself.

Know that with any transition there will be some bumps in the road. That means understanding why you feel a certain way. Re-ignite that spark of hope and promise. Start where you are now and build from there. Your actions and choices will become clearer as you go forward. The good news is that this behavior can be changed when we learn to believe in ourselves and learn from our mistakes. When we admit our mistakes, progress can happen. Before we think about how others might think of us, it is important to think about how much we care about ourselves.

Identifying Your Fears:

Fears are expectations of emotional pain. Don't let these fears stop you from giving your life the best chance to get ahead. No matter how old we are, self-defeating behaviors come from both a fear of success and a fear of failure because of bad experiences in our past. Do any of these fears relate to you?

Fear of disapproval: Do you ask your friends before you try something new? If they reject your idea, do you put it aside? When Joe was a kid, he rarely got approval or encouragement from his parents. As an adult, he makes plans but rarely follows through. He has trouble making decisions and still looks for approval. His memories hold him back from trying anything new. Joe always blamed the world and the people he knew. He could not see his negative thoughts for what they are. His feelings are still attached to old wounds. Those childhood feelings hurt but you don't want to let the people in your past control you now. It helps to understand why you felt a certain way about a past hurt. However, creating it over and over in your mind never allows you to move on and make a better tomorrow.

Fear of success: When something good happens, do you tell yourself, "It was a lucky break" or "I didn't deserve it." Give yourself a "high five" when you do something right. Did you make it work by your persistence and follow-up, by your knowledge and skills, or both?

Fear of rejection: This is one of the worst feelings. It brings on feelings of shock and denial, loss of control (can't change the situation), anger (can't change the past) or blame (I should have_____). Are there things that you avoid? Do you tell yourself, "I was right. If I did that, I would have failed." Instead of putting yourself down, give yourself a fighting chance.

Shame and guilt: There is a difference between shame and guilt.[1] Guilt is feeling bad about what you did. Shame is feeling bad about who you are. Self-criticism is sometimes the cause of feeling that shame. There are some possible strategies for resolving these feelings. Remind yourself of your good qualities. Let out your anger or sadness in a safe way like going for a walk. That helps to relieve the tension that your problem is causing. It's like pressing your "reset" button. Nothing changed, you say? Wrong! You just prevented the power of your fears from hurting you again. Seek support and reassurance from trusted friends and family.

Isolation: Studies have shown that being isolated from others is coping in a negative way.[2] We become immersed in routines, things we do without thinking. Being alone may cause more impulsive behavior. Alcohol or substance abuse ends up imprisoning us further. We find ourselves trapped and it's harder to dig out. A study on isolation found that loneliness and social isolation can shorten our lives. It is as bad as smoking fifteen cigarettes a day. Signs of anxiety include anger or tiredness. Talking to someone is not a waste of time. There are many ways in which our relationships have a protective role. By being with positive friends and people we look up to, we can better cope with the stress in our lives and make better decisions.

Bullying: Bullying is an intentional behavior to humiliate or harm someone. Those who were bullied learned that they were targeted because, in some way, they were different. Michael was picked on from the time he was in elementary school through his high school years.[3] What saved him? He was strong enough to talk to his teacher. He felt overwhelmed and alone but had the courage to take the first step by asking for help. He learned from caring adults that, if you're nice to the bully, it takes away his strength. The bully doesn't expect that reaction. Michael had the confidence to end the situation by talking about his problem.

Henry Winkler, a successful actor, grew up as an angry kid.[4] He was humiliated by his teachers who called him stupid. Now as an adult, he looked back at his life and said: *"Fighting through the bullying gave me the strength that is essential for life."* If you have been verbally abused, stop and ask yourself: "Is that who I am?" Respect yourself. What that person is saying to you is not who you are. Remove yourself from that situation. Set limits. Seek help. Stay calm and balanced. It's not your fault.

People who grow from their traumas are those who are realistic about what went on in their lives. With supportive people around, they can face the problems they have endured and say: "I can build a better life."

Anger: Anger from bad experiences can be carried over for years. Those feelings can control your life now so that you have a hard time moving forward. Here is an example: Tom was talking with a friend who blurted out, "Your folks never paid attention to you, did they?" Tom didn't answer and changed the subject. After thinking about it, he got angry at his friend. A few weeks later, he woke up early. His "a-ha" moment arrived. "Maybe, that's why I snapped at them so much," he thought. Those negative thoughts were subconscious all those years. The key is to talk about your feelings and learn to deal with them so they don't control who you are.

Here is another story of how keeping anger in hurts. **Frank** and his wife were having lunch with friends. The conversation moved from talking about sports to how we were all raised. Out of the blue, he blurted, *"I was abused as a kid by my father."* His mother had the courage to move the family across town. She did cleaning and laundry for other people to bring in some much-needed income. Frank accepted his past with his mother's support and moved on. He said that he felt like a load was taken off his shoulders. He explained that his past no longer holds any power over him. "It's my father's loss," he said.

Letting go of anger can help your health. Anger has been linked to heart disease and other illnesses. When you come from a place of anger or sadness, look at your beliefs and what seems to be true. Is it a fact or your belief about the situation? Your beliefs about yourself are based on who you are, not your appearance or what other people think.

Many people had good intentions, but for various reasons, made poor choices. Whatever the reason, it is not too late. Remind yourself that the decisions you made before do not define who you are now. Your good qualities will give you strength when you learn to trust yourself.

Psychiatrist Viktor Frankl wrote, **"When we are no longer able to change a situation, we are challenged to change ourselves."**[5]

Make room in your thoughts for a new life. Rewrite your story to see it through less pain. Letting go is a way to say that what happened will not hold power over the rest of our lives. It will get easier over time because we will give ourselves permission to make new memories. This does not change the facts. It lets you open your eyes to a new you who is ready to go forward. If you are interested in making some real changes, you need to deal with your issues. We are all going to get old whether we do something or not.

"Moving forward requires positive thinking."[6] More people need to see themselves in a world of possibilities.

David Ortiz, the three time World Series champion, gave the commencement speech to the New England Institute of Technology class of 2017.[7] He focused on the game of life and said:

> "Life is not based on how many times you fail. Life is not based on the people who tell you that you can't. Life is based on what you feel you are capable of doing."

START YOUR STORY

I would describe myself as _____

I am_____

I can_____

My family life is_____

Other influences in my life are_____

Decisions that I made were_____

If I could have chosen a different path, it would be_____

The challenges I face are_____

A better life for me means _____

Picture yourself a few years from now. What do you see? _____

_____

_____

NOTES:

2

WAYS TO COPE

CHAPTER ONE SPOKE ABOUT difficulties in life and understanding the emotions that may be holding you back. Even if it is obvious, it is not easy. This chapter explores strategies to help.

Everyone has memories and feelings that bring us stress. Fortunately, there are strategies to help turn off those self-criticizing thoughts and move forward. If there is an emergency on an airplane, you are told to put the oxygen mask on yourself first. Then help the people around you. This works in day-to-day life too. Help yourself to a better life by working through your issues. Ignoring a problem does not make it go away.

COPING SKILLS:

Coping skills help you recognize what you have to offer. Value yourself. If you heard hurtful words from others, those feelings were learned. They can also be unlearned.

Coping skills help us to be more open-minded. You are not your circumstances. You can create your own, stronger identity. Recognize your barriers. Understand your blind-spots (what you don't want to know). It is important to know what is true.

Coping is learning to see the other person's point of view. Coping is being able to see realities more clearly. It is learning to rely on others who are strong where we are not.

Coping helps us to deal with our negative thoughts and feelings. It is used to reduce stress from our problems, difficulties and everyday situations. They tell us that we have gone through bad times and have survived. Coping thoughts help when we feel nervous, angry or sad.

> ✎ *You can handle your feelings:*
>
> **When we are aware of our feelings, we have an easier time learning to calm down. Think of a situation that upset you. How did you handle it?**

McKay, Davis and Fanning, authors of "Thoughts and Feelings,"[1] suggest using these coping skills when we are feeling edgy:

1. My thoughts do not control my life. I am in charge of my thoughts.

2. I am nervous but can deal with the situation.

3. I can ride this out and not let it get to me.

4. I am learning to cope with my anxieties.

5. I am a good person. I can do better.

6. Everyone makes mistakes. No one is perfect.

7. I survived bad times. I will get through this too.

When we start to balance how we see a situation and our emotions, we usually see it as just either good or bad. There are actually three sides to every story. The first side is the best story: (I've got it made). The second side is the worst: (there is nothing good about my story). The third one is more likely to be closer to the truth (some parts of the story are good and other parts are bad). It is realistic. When you look at a situation, look at your point of view. Then, try to put yourself in the other person's shoes. Ask yourself:

What happened? _____

_____

Why did it happen? _____

_____

What is that other person's position? _____

_____

What did he or she do to make me think that? _____

_____

The point is to separate your feelings from the actual event. Instead of jumping to a wrong conclusion, you get to the heart of the issue to find a solution. You need to understand that nothing stays the same. When you come up with your own coping thoughts, you get through what is bothering you right now.

You need to be aware of your emotions. If you feel uncomfortable in a situation, walk away. When you say "no," mean it. Take care of you. Is there a person or a group that makes you feel unhappy in any way? There are no rules that require toxic situations to continue. Choose to be with people who care about you.

In some communities, there are only a few programs to offer assistance with parenting, childcare and other issues. For young mothers, their problems began with peer pressure or low self-esteem. Sometimes, it is a lack of parental guidance or positive role models. There is a true story of a girl at a young age in South Carolina whose life had been filled with poverty and disappointments.[2] She had five children with five different men and was abused by each one. Years later, she heard of Job Corps, a training program, from a neighbor. With encouragement, she earned a high school diploma, gained work experience and learned how to budget. She said that she sees things differently now. Her new knowledge and her daughters' achievements in school have encouraged her to carry on. Her oldest daughter said: "We've been through too much. I am grateful for all things we have. Life is hard and I want to go to school and be successful."

Some who do not have your best interest at heart might put pressure on you to say "yes." You know that it would be a bad decision. Chances are, your more rational side will tell you to walk away and cool down. When you take better care of yourself, your ability to control your own behavior becomes stronger. You learn to resist impulsive or risky behaviors. Show courage and create a new destiny.

Be aware of your thoughts about the situation. Is there any evidence that challenges those thoughts? It is OK to see that some of your behavior needs to change. If you feel disrespected by someone, there are several ways to deal with the situation:

a) You could ignore it. The problem with this approach is that "it will eat at you." The stress inside will build until you might explode.

b) You could confront that person. The problem is that you don't know the limits of the other party. It could lead to an ugly situation with violence and physical pain.

c) A better choice is to deal with that person without escalating the situation. How? Look at that person. In a strong voice, say that his/her actions are not OK and move on. If you accept verbal abuse to keep things OK, you could be robbing yourself of your potential.

People act out because their feelings drive them. When upset, take a moment and calm down. Acknowledge how you feel. Use your coping skills. Interrupt your negative thoughts by distracting yourself. For example, listen to music. It's natural for us to get upset once in a while. If you made a mistake, say to yourself, "I will do better and not make the same mistake again." We can't change something until we acknowledge that it's there. When we accept responsibility, we can move on. That is why it is so important to learn how to manage our feelings.

Here is an example of how to cope with stressful situations more effectively:

Old way: We argued.

Consequences: We both stayed angry for weeks.

New way of coping: I can be in better control of my emotions.

Better possible consequences: I can walk away and feel stronger.

THE LIFE YOU HAVE LED DOESN'T NEED TO BE
THE ONLY LIFE YOU HAVE"

-ANNE QUINDLEN

Situations happen that are beyond our control. The situation is your reality today. It is not your future. When you accept the situation for what it is, you can reduce your over-reaction or strong emotional response. Are your decisions helping or hurting you? You get satisfaction in the moment when you think "I drink but it's not hurting anyone" but it is. It could take years off your life expectancy.

Whatever the situation is, you need to judge if the price you are paying is worth it to you. You cannot change what happened but you can change your reaction to the situation. Stay in control rather than over-reacting. One of the reasons people get into a "funk" could be the hidden emotions that they don't want to face. It is just too painful. "You upset me!" Or "You made me do it!" These are survival responses. Just because you feel that way does not mean that it is a fact. Realize that you are not your emotions. You can still feel your emotions but not be controlled by them.

WAYS TO MANAGE YOUR EMOTIONS MORE EFFECTIVELY

Learning To Forgive:

Forgiveness helps to make us less angry. Those memories might have framed your actions as an adult. Are you acting in a way that keeps those bad feelings alive? Are those fears driving your emotions now? Are you trying to hide your pain? Take the first step and recognize the hurt. What is it doing to you? Your emotions can be your friend or your enemy. The most important thing to remember is that you cannot control what happened in the past. What you can control is your reaction to the event. Start by thinking how you could move on from a misunderstanding. Focus on something good. Forgiveness happens gradually. The rewards we gain from forgiveness are bigger than holding in that hurt.

Life always has setbacks. No one escapes. The challenge is learning how to get ahead. Don't let your self-beliefs hold you back. A few behavioral changes make a big difference on how you see things now. When you pay attention to your emotions, you will become more aware. Then you can put the brakes on your outbursts and learn strategies to help stay in control.

Listening:

It's hard to really listen when you feel that parts of you are not good enough.[3] People argue because they think you don't hear them. The point is not to cut the other person off. How we react makes all the difference. Saying things that you might regret is not OK Even if you apologize, the words are still in the other person's mind. Don't increase the anger by saying things like "you always_____." Are you a listener who gets defensive? Can you accept criticism? Can you respect the other person's point of view? Try concentrating on the complaint. Ask yourself: what else is that person trying to say? Put it in your own words: "Are you saying _____?" When you learn to respect the other person's feelings, you also learn to treat your own feelings with respect.

Problems don't solve themselves. Talk through small problems before they get out of hand. Here are some phrases to help cool down the emotions in a disagreement:

- This is important, please listen.
- I never thought of it that that before.

- Try to understand my point of view.

Here is an example of you, as a good listener:

When someone says: *"I had a bad day."*

You could say: *"You sound pretty down. Tell me about what happened."*

Those non–judgmental comments make the other person feel supported and listened to. Communication is a two-way street.

When you open yourself up to new possibilities, you can create a better future. Pay attention to the good things that happen. Look for something that you handled well and give yourself credit.

Self-compassion:

Self-compassion is learning to feel good about ourselves.[4]

Self-compassion has three parts:

1) self-kindness

2) understanding that negative experiences are part of each person's life

3) accepting those painful thoughts and feelings. Putting your finger on the cause of your feelings might keep you from re-hashing it over and over.

To stop replaying a situation in your head, take a few minutes and focus on a small achievement, something that you feel good about.

🖉   *Keep a self-compassion diary:*

One step forward is to keep a self-compassion diary. When you focus on what you accomplished, you are motivating yourself more than you realize. Just jot down the good things you did daily. Keep it next to your bed or desk. Just a few sentences will help. It's a mood changer. Here is an example: I did _____ to help myself today.

Please get help if you feel out of control. It could change your life. Getting help early is better than letting a situation get out of hand. These sites connect people with licensed mental health professionals via video chats, text messages and phone calls.

Check out:

BetterHelp.com

TalkSpace.com

GoodTherapy.org

Or, contact a psychologist, social worker or counselor near you.

WAYS I COPE

Think of a situation where you reacted_____

Why did it happen?_____

How did you feel? _____

What did you say or do? _____

Was your reaction good or upsetting?_____

Are there positive things about that situation? _____

_____

My coping strategy is: _____

_____

What can you do to change your mood to focus on what you want? _____

_____

What advice would you give to yourself now? _____

_____

What do you like about yourself? _____

_____

NOTES:

3

Be Mindful

MINDFULNESS AND HAPPINESS: Is there a connection? In the last chapter, we spoke about the value of using coping skills to be more in control of your emotions. In this chapter, you will learn another way to control stress: mindfulness.

Mindfulness means "being in the present moment."[1] It makes you stronger and helps keep you calmer under pressure. It helps to clear out thoughts that are getting in the way of seeing things more clearly. The power to heal yourself is in the ability to think of now, not then.

"You can't stop the waves...

But you can learn to surf"

    - Jon Kabat-Zinn, who coined the phrase "mindfulness"

Mindfulness Helps To Decrease Anxiety And Manage Your Emotions.

Many people suffer in silence. A small event could lead to an upsetting day. When stressed, how do you behave? Do you end up blaming yourself? Reacting in ways that hurt your health could increase your stress. That's why it is important to get a handle on those issues before anxiety gets out of hand. Mindfulness helps to manage your emotions, decrease anxiety and creates a better way to manage your choices.

Mindfulness worked for the U.S. Marines.[2] If it worked for the Marines, it could work for you. Four platoons were trained on an eight-week mindfulness program plus standard combat training. The other four platoons received only the standard combat training.

Their training required all the Marines to go through a mock situation where one group was "ambushed" and very stressed. The second group was not "ambushed." Both groups had their brains scanned before and after the study. The results showed that the Marines who were trained in mindfulness had their heart rates return to normal faster than those who did not have that additional training. The changes showed that those Marines who had the mindfulness training learned to deal with stress better. The study has implications to help those with PTSD (Post Traumatic Stress Disorder) and trauma.

How Mindfulness Helps:

Mindfulness reduces stress and anxiety. It gives you time to think about how to respond to a certain situation.[3] Recognizing an action does not mean reacting to it. It allows you to be responsible and think of the consequences. You are making a choice so you will not be a victim of impulse. When you practice mindfulness, you are less likely to "blow up" and let that grudge control your thoughts. Mindfulness helps to keep the anger under control so you don't have to act on those feelings. When you learn to forgive and let go of that resentment, you can concentrate on your own personal growth. Mindfulness helps your overall ability to manage your emotions and decrease your anxiety. It helps to keep you calm under pressure.

Mindfulness works by slowing you down for a few minutes. The value of slowing down and breathing is that when negative thoughts occur, you observe and let them go. The simple act of paying attention to your thoughts helps to control your reactions. It gives you a clearer focus to improve what you are doing. It creates a way to help you progress so you can make better choices. The first step is to be aware of your emotions. Pay attention. Recognize where those feelings came from. Be in the present instead of re-living what happened in the past again. This helps you to make reasonable choices instead of impulsive choices. We can not change how our past influenced who we are. Your past is not your future. Neither avoidance nor denial will help. What we can control is how we respond to our present time—now.

Mindfulness makes you stronger. It can help improve your performance at work, in sports, and other events. It creates a way to get you progress and make better choices. Newscaster and author Dan Harris wrote several books[4] on mindfulness. He said that "mindfulness makes you more insightful. The real gift of mindfulness is directing your attention to the present. It works to clear our mind. It gives us more focus and control over our emotions by recognizing the patterns that change our mood. It gives us space between our impulses and actions so we don't react to every thought that pops into our heads."

How To practice mindfulness:

How do you practice mindfulness? Here is a guide. Find a quiet place. Sit in a comfortable position and close your eyes. Take some deep breaths. Breathe in from your diaphragm and breathe out slowly from your nose. Feel cool air coming in and warm air leaving your nostrils. When you slowly let go of each breath, you are releasing mental tension and physical stress. You observe and let it go. Your heart rate will slow down and, with time, stress will ease up. Aim for three minutes at a time. If you get distracted, just start again.

When to practice mindfulness. A good time to practice mindfulness is just before you go to bed. It only takes a few minutes. The benefit is that it calms you down for a better night's sleep. Remember, you don't change your reality. Accept that your past is your past. Your road to calmness is paved with self-acceptance. Your future is in front of you. Don't waste your time so wrapped up in past grudges or so worried about the future that the present fails to get our attention. Our present time is a gift.

Consistency is important. Make it a habit. People who practice mindfulness make better decisions because they are calmer and can think things through. You can practice mindfulness when you are going for a walk or sitting still. Give it a try. Don't pressure yourself. The calmer you are, the more likely it will work for you. Many studies have shown that the part of the brain that triggers negative emotions has reduced reactions when mindfulness is practiced. Instead of focusing on your stressful thoughts, focus on your surroundings. Just notice.

How to be Happy:

Happiness: Is there such a thing? Happiness means different things to different people. It is more of a general feeling of contentment, but somewhat fleeting. This helps you deal with what life brings you. One of the strongest goals is to make peace with the kind of life you are building. In his book, *Oneness with All Life*, author Eckhart Tolle said "that the primary cause of unhappiness is never the situation but your thoughts about the situation."[5]

There are the facts and then there are the thoughts. Those thoughts about the situation limit you from taking action steps. Sometimes expectations drive our unhappiness. These expectations could be from people in our lives, or certain events from our past. It takes some hard knocks to gain the maturity to sort things out and carry out a plan. Happiness is somewhere between pleasure and what is meaningful to you. Make sure that you have some activities to give you both during the week. Happiness is compromised by exhausting yourself. Regular exercise, a better diet and enough sleep lead to better physical and mental health. When you hear your favorite song or when you open a gift, you feel joy. The feeling is strong even though it does not last a long time. Those moments should be treasured.

Happiness And Gratitude:

There is a strong connection between happiness and gratitude. To find happiness, you need to remember to look for it.[6] Small things make a difference. Is there anything that you take for granted? Be grateful for what you have. Focus on the positive. Associate yourself with grateful people. Never compare. Start small. Practice mindfulness. Keep your mind on now instead of what happened before that has been bothering you. Give thanks. People who notice what they are grateful for each day are happier than those who don't. Think about what you are looking forward to. Work on something you like to do: hobby, sports, etc. Be aware of how you feel when you relax and enjoy what you are doing.

✎   *Start a Gratitude Journal*

A gratitude journal helps to remind you of the good things. Keeping a daily or weekly journal of what went right leaves you feeling less stressed and more optimistic about the future. Write down a few things that went well. They might be small like "lunch was good" or "I got a phone call from an old friend." See everyday things or events as gifts and enjoy the good feelings that come with them.

BE MINDFUL

What are you grateful for? _____

_____

What does happiness look like for you? _____

_____

Friends: _____

_____

Family: _____

_____

Health: _____

_____

Work: _____

_____

Hobbies: _____

_____

What do you do to calm yourself? _____

_____

What do you look forward to? _____

_____

"LIFE ISN'T WAITING FOR THE WIND TO CHANGE.

IT'S LEARNING HOW TO ADJUST YOUR SAILS."

-Author unknown

NOTES:

4

THE VALUE OF A MENTOR

IN THE LAST CHAPTER we spoke about ways to balance how you see a situation and your emotions. Making changes in life is not easy. Having someone in your corner really helps.

Having someone on your side is a good idea. A mentor is an ally to help you move toward the life you want. That person will help you grow personally and professionally. The mentor will listen to your thoughts, concerns and ideas in a respectful way. He or she will share his or her knowledge with you and will be an advocate to help reach your goals.

Do you believe that you have more value than you are showing now? Are you settling for less than what you need or want? You will feel that control is back in your hands when you develop a plan. Part of the plan is to connect with a mentor. Seeking out a mentor is a sign of strength, not weakness. The purpose of having a mentor is to gain insight and knowledge.

> **Dave** grew up without a father and had run-ins with the law.[1] With the help of the prison chaplain, he went back to school. He decided that he wanted to work as a chaplain to help prisoners. He said that "the only difference between the prisoners and us is that they made some really bad choices." He was asked why he made the sacrifice of time and money to do this work. He said, "just one life changed is worth it."

A pattern of not working up to your capability can be fueled by growing up in an environment that doesn't encourage success, by a lack of opportunities or a lack of positive people in your life. Here is a true story of how a mentor changed a boy's life for the better. A boy told a friend that he would never go to college because his family did drugs.[2] He was thinking of running away. One day, that boy was on a bus. A man sat next to him and they got to talking and connected. That man became his mentor. With encouragement, the boy later joined the Achievers Program at the YMCA. They bring in speakers who talk about their challenges and their success. That boy went from failing in school to becoming an honor roll student. To see if there is a Y Achievers program near you, search for "Y Achievers + a city near you".

There are several important points that can reverse the pattern of not working up to one's abilities. One is working with a strong role model or mentor who can encourage and motivate you. Next, create a disciplined lifestyle. The daily structure will help you learn good habits. It also works to help you discover your strengths. Athletes gain confidence when mentored by their coach. You are more likely to stick with positive changes when there is someone on your side. It is so important to feel encouraged.

> **Jeff** came from a broken home.[3] The fast food restaurant employees where he worked after school became his substitute family. He had no support at home and didn't know where to start to better his life. At work, the path to doing well was clear. Work hard and do things right. He said that, for the first time in his life, he felt empowered. His shift leader was like a father figure and encouraged him to go to college. One evening he told Jeff to stop working, get his scholarship application in the overnight mail and handed Jeff the money for postage. Jeff ended up going to that school and learned that he can succeed.

There is a strong connection between your motivation and what you do. Motivation grows with the belief that you can actually do whatever you need to, to reach your goals. When we tell someone that we are going to do something, and we have to report back, we put in more effort to make sure we will follow through. Some mentors have offered this advice: let go of your mistakes, take advantage of any good opportunity, and have a back-up plan. Having a mentor is important, helps spur you on, and is a good sounding board. You gain by discussing your goals, options, and the direction in which you want to go. There is nothing more helpful than talking about your daily wins and setbacks. Have someone who listens and gives you constructive feedback.

How to Find a Mentor:

Here are some suggestions to find a mentor. Think about people you respect for their common sense and knowledge. Who would you want to be like? Think of an industry you are interested in. Look at people that you know in your area. Odds are, you might already know someone who would be a good fit. Look at specific areas such as owners of small businesses or people who work in a field that that you are interested in.

Think of someone that you can learn from. Could this person be a realistic cheerleader to encourage you? Do you feel comfortable speaking with him or her? Does your gut say, "This is a good fit." You might already know someone who could be a great help, even though you never thought of that person in that way before. That person could even be younger than you. A "figure it out together" kind of person would be a good mentor. You could also go to community events on careers, job fairs, and trade shows. You might be introduced to someone or you might meet someone in passing. There are also many nonprofit organizations that may offer help at no charge to you.

Don't be put off by people that you think are better than you. You could gain a better focus on how to grow, learn specific skills, and get along better with others at work. You are sending a message to a possible mentor that you think enough of yourself that you want to improve at _____ (whatever you're reaching for).

There is strength in letting yourself grow in different ways, especially when a strong support person has your back. It's natural for us to feel uncomfortable asking for assistance. Look at it this way. The other person might be flattered and happy to be of help.

You could call and say, "I am very interested in the field of _____. Could we meet to discuss this? I would like to learn more information about _____. When would be a good time to meet? To prepare for the meeting, think about how you would like the potential mentor to help. It is your responsibility to keep the connection going, once he or she agrees to be your mentor.

You Found A Mentor. Now What?

Be prepared for the first meeting. Keep expectations realistic. Have a list of questions prepared that tell your potential mentor of your interests, goals and expectations. What areas would you like to work on in follow-up meetings? How often would you meet? After the meeting, it is a good idea to call or write a thank you note. No need to use the word "mentor." It is the professional relationship that is important. You are looking for someone who agrees to guide you with his or her knowledge and experience about your career choice. You want someone who is caring and can be honest with you.

It is motivating to have someone on your side who can ask good questions such as: "What do you think you might do differently?" The conversations can narrow down your options and identify what is important to you. Ask questions relating to the discussion you had. The person you met with will learn what you are thinking about and be able to offer direction. The meetings can give information about an industry or jobs in that field.

When Larry could not decide what he wanted to do in life, he spoke to his mentor. The mentor said, "Stop putting yourself down. You have skills. You will learn from your experiences and continue to improve. Let's look at where your best opportunities might be." The mentor's role is to advise, guide and suggest. Your role is to do the work and follow through with any suggestions or plans.

Listening is not easy, especially if you are speaking with someone you don't know well.[4] Do not make the mistake of not really listening. Look at the person speaking, not the floor. Nod your head and add an occasional, "I understand." Do not interrupt. Think about the other person's point of view. Respond in a way that the other person knows you are paying attention. Focus on what the other person is talking about. Then, ask questions to get the other person to talk. You can learn from his or her experience.

The mentor is not judgmental. The mentor offers understanding and motivation throughout this process. He or she is an advocate and will support you as you make changes and find your direction. It is important that you respect this person for his or her common sense and knowledge in the industries that you are considering.

The mentor's experience can give you information that you might not be aware of. That can help you get a clearer focus on what you want to do in life, learn specific skills, gain insight about appropriate business behavior and keep your expectations realistic. It is important to make a commitment. Don't make the mistake of quitting after the first few meetings with your mentor. If you do, you'll be back to being stuck. Be respectful of the mentor's time and knowledge. There is nothing more helpful than discussing your day with a supportive listener. When you do that, it will be a "win-win" situation.

The Value Of A Mentor:

1. What do you expect to gain from having a mentor? _____

_____

      Support: _____

      Confidence-building: _____

      Challenge me to reach my goals: _____

      Advice: _____

2. What would you like to talk about with your mentor? _____

_____

      Career options: _____

      Job readiness: _____

      Specific skills: _____

      How to network and get job leads: _____

      Help me with job opportunities: _____

3. How do you think that a mentor can help? _____

_____

4. What support do you want from a mentor? _____

_____

5. Who do you respect? _____

_____

6. Who would you like to follow to be more successful? _____

_____

7. Who would help you to be accountable? _____

_____

8. My list of possible mentors is:

Name:	Date contacted:	Result	Follow-up
_____	_____	_____	_____
_____	_____	_____	_____
_____	_____	_____	_____

Meeting With Your Mentor:

What qualities do you want your mentor to know about you? _____

_____

_____

List two or three goals you would like to work on: _____

_____

_____

_____

What challenges do you face in your daily life? _____

_____

How do you wish your life to be in six months to a year from now? _____

_____

I will ask my mentor about: _____

_____

Our next meeting date will be: _____

We will discuss: _____

I want my mentor to guide me in: _____

_____

Ask your mentor, "Can you help me figure out...?" _____

_____

_____

_____

NOTES:

5

You Have Potential

IN THE LAST CHAPTER, we spoke about the value of having a mentor on your side. This chapter will talk about ways you can look at your habits and learn to be more focused.

The secret of getting ahead is simple. It is: getting started. You are the one you are waiting for. Remember, you are competing against your old self. Give yourself another chance. Transformation is possible. Be ready to change. Be stubborn (in a good way) to carve out a better life for you and your family. Finding your power means being with people who will act as good advisors. You will gain the strength and energy to move your life forward.

George was the oldest in his family.[1] The family moved around a lot, so he learned how to make friends quickly. When he was fifteen, his dad died suddenly. He did not rise to the occasion to be "the man of the house." Instead, he wanted to escape his pain. He made some bad decisions and got in with the wrong crowd. He was arrested. After doing time, he traveled down south. He became proficient on the guitar and supported himself with gigs. He learned his lesson and chose friends that helped him. Many years later, he said that he now feels okay about himself. George said: "You can't control what happens to you. The only thing you can control is how you deal with it."

RESISTING CHANGE:

Be aware of your resistance to change. Ask yourself, what am I giving up? It's easier to put whatever you are doing on hold to avoid feeling defeated. When you see that you're not giving up much and that life can be better, you are ready to move forward. Meet with your support team (mentor and friends). Brainstorm. Talking it over is a motivator. Change is possible when we are clear about what we want the outcome to be. For example, if you want to lose weight, it's not enough to say, "I will eat less." You could get too hungry and then eat the wrong kind of food. A better way is to follow a diet that will give you the nutrition needed to stick with the plan.

Do one thing at a time. Break the task into smaller parts. Keep going each day to get the job done. People who do this build confidence and develop a stronger ability to deal with stress. Every little step will get you closer to completing the job you set out to do. Focus and stay in control. Talk with your mentor to come up with some suggestions to make those goals more manageable.

Bad habits can hurt you. These habits might be: taking shortcuts, leaving things until the last minute then rushing through the job, not putting in a steady effort, having trouble making decisions, not finishing what you started or doubting yourself. Research has shown that people usually underestimate the work needed to get their job done. You have to believe that your efforts will allow you to accomplish your task.

Putting things off is a bad habit. It's easy to think of a dozen excuses such as "I'll do it tomorrow." Tomorrow comes and there is another reason. Does this sound like you? Do you procrastinate? When you are unsure of how to do something, that uncertainty could stop you from trying. Avoidance of a job you don't like is not a good idea. It usually makes matters worse. How badly do you want it? One way to fight putting things off is to set small tasks that are achievable. Identify what you want to accomplish. Make sure it is a realistic goal.

It takes some determination and awareness of what it takes to get a job done. If you have to be somewhere at a certain time, you would have to start your day earlier. That will give you enough time to get ready and be at your meeting without the stress of running late.

The difference between getting things done (productivity) or "I'll do it tomorrow" (procrastination), said Charles Duhigg, the author of *Smarter, Faster, Better,* said,

"Anyone can learn to be more productive. It's not about being smarter. It's about learning to control your focus and picking the right goals."[2] He goes on to say that "feeling like you are in control is critical to trigger your motivation (productivity). Otherwise, you're just reacting to things. When you feel in control, you decide what motivates you and what to focus on." Duhigg continues: "Sometimes you just need to make a choice. Think of organizing your day and deciding what to do first. You need to ask yourself which task matters more.

These questions are not ridiculous. You are training your brain to know what to focus on and what to be motivated about. When you react to something, like a phone call, you lose focus on what you were doing. To get back on track, think about what is most important. Ignore distractions. The truth is: making good choices is a good way to help yourself. Think of a habit you want to form. It is never too late to change your way of doing things. Your new way becomes stronger with repetition. It takes about three weeks to become accustomed to a new habit. Change one thing at a time. Replace the bad habit with a good habit. This is your commitment to yourself to make lasting changes.

Be more aware of what you do daily. Your actions affect you and the people who care about you. Be aware of your health. Don't ignore any pains or problems. If yesterday was not a good day, get back on track today. Learn how to deal with obstacles by deciding which options might work best to solve those problems. When you think about what you want to accomplish, you become more productive. Give yourself credit for what you do.

Be aware of your decisions, both short and long-term. When you are set in your ways and believe you cannot change, it is called a fixed mindset.[3] An example is saying: "I'm just not good at it" without even trying. A growth mindset means looking at things with a more open mind. Instead of saying, "I'm not good at _____, reframe your thoughts or feelings to "I just haven't learned how to do it yet but I will." Think about what you need to know. Believe that you can improve with more effort. No one is perfect. We all make mistakes. When you pick yourself up, you give yourself another opportunity. If your first plan did not work out say, "I will figure out what I need to do." Plan your next steps. Setbacks happen to everyone. Setbacks are not forever. Remember: give yourself one small accomplishment each day. Don't think about what you didn't do but focus on what you did. If you think you must be perfect, you never will satisfy yourself. Give yourself a fighting chance.

> The story of **Norma Heath** was reported in WCVB news as: "Woman goes from Homeless to Harvard University." [4] Norma's story tells of the hardships in her life. She went from living in the streets to staying at Rosie's Place, a homeless shelter in Boston. There, she learned the power of goal setting. She was required to write down her goals every week. One week, it was "keep my doctor's appointment." With counseling, she stretched to reach her goals and learned to become more optimistic about her future. One day, the counselor asked her what her goals were. She had a hard time answering. She never had goals, except to survive. She surprised herself and answered, "I want to go to Harvard University." She took one course at a time at Harvard's extension program. In June, 2017, she graduated.

"IT'S ALL ABOUT GOALS. YOU CAN HAVE YOUR DREAMS BUT THERE'S A DIFFERENCE BETWEEN DREAMS AND GOALS."

- Norma Heath

YOU HAVE POTENTIAL

What separates those who do from those who don't? Those who reach for their goals never give up. Your personal strength will grow with optimism based on realistic expectations.

What is your attitude when you need to solve a problem?

- It's difficult: _____

- It takes some work: _____

- With time, I'll get it right: _____

My overall attitude is: _____

_____

My hopes and aspirations are: _____

_____

What I really want in life is: _____

_____

The habit I want to change: _____

_____

The new habit that I will make: _____

_____

What else can I do to keep going? _____

_____

NOTES:

6

What Do You Want? The Power of Choice

I N CHAPTER FIVE, WE spoke about goals and habits to keep moving forward. In this chapter, you will learn to make a plan tailored to your strengths, interests, values and skills.

Starting over doesn't mean that you are starting from scratch. You have skills. You have overcome challenges and are moving ahead. Mark Cuban, entrepreneur on the TV show *Shark Tank,* said it this way, "**It's not where you came from but where you are going.**"

Take Stock of Your Successes:

Look at what you have done and what things you enjoy doing. Instead of saying, "It happened to me," look at your life differently. Challenge these negative thoughts. Say, "I choose to..." This simple change puts you in charge and in control of going for the result that you want.

"I choose to have a job where I can _____

"I choose to take a path to become a _____

Wanting gets you nowhere. Choosing gets you the results that you want. Realistically, look at your lifestyle now. Change is hard to make until you see your own truth. If you keep doing what you always do, you will get what you have gotten before. That is OK in certain things. But it is not OK when you are looking to change. When our thoughts become repetitive, it is hard to break that pattern. For example, if you got a bad grade in math class when you were younger, you might avoid math now. You might not have been paying attention then. Unless you challenge your beliefs, you might go through life without giving yourself a chance to do something you like.

It is normal to hesitate when you don't know what to expect. What would your success look like? I am not talking about winning the lottery. If you could start a new career, what do you think it might be? How would you picture your new life? Many people have moved from not doing what they are capable of to feeling proud of how far they have come.

Each person turned their life into what he or she wanted because each had a plan and worked with one or more mentors. They became more aware of their habits and the choices they were making. They learned that their thoughts can work for or against them. The journey is worth the challenges. Allow change to take place.

The decisions you make will help build your life from the ground up – with a stronger foundation. Are you willing to reach out? It is never too late. What personal sacrifices do you think you will have to make? Identifying these issues will help you make better decisions based on awareness. The information you discover about yourself will clarify your choices and make you more productive. There are no shortcuts. Each step backwards is a lesson to tweak your approach. Life moves on by trial and error. You move forward by motivation and focus, good mentors, possible classes and training. Give yourself permission to succeed.

> **Sean** was a kid who got picked on a lot. By chance, someone gave him tickets to see a bodybuilding show.[1] His mother said that she never saw him so excited about anything before. From that day on, he used bodybuilding to change his life. He said, "When you change your attitude, you change your mind. When you change your mind, you change your life." He said that by sheer work, force of will and a belief in himself, he did it. He is now a police lieutenant and proud of what he has accomplished for himself and for the community.

Assess Your Strengths:

Each of us has strengths. Our best qualities might have been hidden but they are still there. You didn't lose them. Your job is to recognize the strengths that you have. You don't have to start completely over. Use those strengths that match your skills, talents and values.

Keep an open mind. You can succeed at the realistic goals you choose but it takes work and focus. The sections in this chapter will help you to make an informed decision for your next opportunity. Consider your needs, interests, and goals. A career decision, based on your strengths and your individual qualities, is a better decision. When you like what you do, you keep at it and become better at doing that type of work. To give you a better chance of success, you need to identify your special qualities.

Talents are the natural abilities that you were born with. These talents give each person a special ability and stay with you for your entire life. You create a strength when your natural talents are made stronger with practice. For example, a musician gets better with rehearsals and by applying the lessons learned in music class. You can get better at your career choice when you use your strengths and apply them with training to achieve success. A person can have strengths in more than one area. Our interests and talents develop and change throughout our lives.

Your **personality-type** is your unique way of thinking, behaving or reacting. Personality-type does not measure intelligence. It describes you. The people who are most comfortable in their jobs are the ones who are in careers that match their personality. It is doing what comes naturally to you and not forced on you. A personality-type book titled *Do What You Are* by Paul and Barbara Baron-Tieger, can be used to identify your personality type, your strengths and weaknesses, and possible career options.[2] Write down your most important personality traits, such as quiet or outgoing, problem-solver, organized, dependable, etc. Use this information as a tool to narrow your choices. Trust your gut, advice from your mentor, and those people who know you well and have your best interests at heart. A librarian might be able to get the book or you can find it online at PersonalityType.com

Skills are learned abilities like carpentry, mechanics, or any other learned skill. The book *Discover What You're Best At*, by Linda Gale, divides all jobs into 41 career groups and divides each skills cluster into jobs and the education required for each job.[3] It suggests several career directions to consider. Create a list of potential occupations that use those skills. Cross off any skills you do not enjoy doing. The information you gain will help give you the words to explain your strengths at a job interview.

YOUR SKILLS

Use this worksheet to identify the skills you want to use or learn for your career. Check the skills that are important to you at a job:

5 – most important; 4 or 3 – somewhat important; or 2 or 1 – least important

Artistic __   Athletic __   Bilingual __

Dexterity __   Eye-hand coordination __   Interpersonal skills __

Instruction/teaching __   Investigation/Fact-Finding __ Logical thinking __

Mathematical __   Attention to detail ___   Outdoor work __

Sales/negotiations __ Scientific __   Writing Skills __

Supervising/leadership __ Verbal communication skills __

Other skills not listed __

Problem solving skills such as: getting the facts, trouble-shooting, testing ideas and diagnosing the problem.

Organizational skills such as: calculating an estimate, keeping deadlines, organizing records, and accepting responsibility.

Look at your skills that can be applied to any work environment, such as your attention to details. Employers are looking to hire people who will be an asset to their company. Training a new employee costs the firm money. Thus, they want someone who will stay with the firm and fits into the company culture. Important attitudes include: being a good worker, always on time, a problem-solver, well-liked (friendly), being organized and adaptable to different situations.

Interests: There has to be something in your life that makes you want to get up in the morning. What would you do if you could start over?_____

_____

What words would you use to describe yourself? _____

_____

What is the quality about yourself that you feel good about? _____

_____

Are there any hobbies that you really like to do? _____

_____

    Values: Values are principles or qualities that you consider important. There are personal values and there are also work values.

PERSONAL VALUES:

What were your values growing up? _____

_____

What life experiences made you feel good? _____

_____

What things are important to you now? _____

_____

_____

What people do you look up to (coaches, teachers, family, friends)? _____

_____

How do these values fit in with your priorities? Try to honestly answer these questions. Next, look at what you value at work. Think about what will make you happy on the job:

WORK VALUES:

Check how you rate them:	Important	Not So Much
Variety on the job:	____	____
Steady job:	____	____
Fast-paced:	____	____
Supervision:	____	____
Contact with the public:	____	____
Work alone:	____	____
Work on a team:	____	____
Desk job:	____	____
Working outdoors:	____	____

What else is important to you? _____

_____

What salary do you need to make ends meet? $_____

Do you need flexible hours? _____Can you put in overtime? _____

_____

How far are you willing to commute? _____

Can you relocate? _____

Do you have a passion to do something that you have dreamed about? _____

_____

Are you willing to put in the preparation and time to get to the career you want? ___

_____

GO WITH YOUR STRENGTHS.

Consider your temperament, skills and abilities. Your answers will help to learn more about yourself. You can set specific job objectives once your target areas are identified. You know what skills you can offer a company, what salary range you can live on, the level of responsibility you want, how far you are willing to travel, and the type of industry you would like to work in.

The website: Onet.org is a good resource to learn more about careers. Check out the six sections on their site.

- "Bright Outlook" lists occupations that are projected to grow rapidly between 2018 and 2024.

- The section "Tools" lists related jobs that someone might be interested in. Here is an example of how the site can be used. Steve knew how to use a power router tool but did not want to be a bench carpenter. He wanted to know what other jobs used power routers. He typed in "power routers" and these jobs using power routers came up: cabinet makers; cement masons; construction carpenters; and drywall, ceiling and flooring installers. He then looked at jobs he was interested in within his commuting area.

- "Job Zone" lists job titles by category - no preparation, some preparation, considerable or extensive preparation and "expand your options." Check out the possibilities. You might consider looking into careers that are related to the one that you worked in.

- "Interest Profiler explores possible occupations based on the job skills and job-related activities that appeal to you."

- "Abilities Profiler identifies strengths and the occupations that match those strengths."

- "Work Importance pinpoints what is important to you in a job."

Know yourself. An optimistic outlook and persistence are important. We all have strengths and weaknesses. Our abilities and our focus determine what we can do. Set realistic goals. Choose a career path in a field that is hiring and that matches your skills and personality.

> **Mike** wanted to feel useful. He needed an income, wanted to try something different, and knew he had back-up skills. He was not sure about learning new skills. He spoke with his mentor, someone that he used to work with. Mike narrowed his options to welding or electrical work. His next step was to talk with people in those fields.

His mentor helped him to see that:

a) He handled machinery well.

b) He liked the work environment.

c) He had good people skills.

d) He could get part-time work while he trained for a new career.

What jobs or careers could use your skills? Do these choices match your strengths? Some will be crossed off quickly. Others will look better as you match them with reality. One or two choices will remain. When you talk it over, use your practical information and knowledge to make a better decision. Don't cross out a career or a job because you don't have the experience. For example, a building contractor may be taking on an apprentice to learn HVAC (heating, ventilation, and air conditioning). You might get a good opportunity for on-the-job training. With a successful job performance and passing the test, you could become certified and have a good career.

Jot down your skills and abilities, those things you feel you do well: _____

_____

How have you used them at work: _____

_____

Create a list of possible jobs or the type of work you want to do: _____

_____

Think about the work environment of that career. Do you feel it would be something that you could enjoy long-term? _____

_____

Do you know anyone doing that work? Take the time to meet that person and ask good questions: _____

Does your job choice match your personal and work values? _____

_____

What are the advantages? _____

_____

_____

What are the risks? _____

_____

Does your gut tell you if it is a good fit? _____

_____

Use these questions to guide you:

Skills I really enjoy: _____

_____

Skills I am good at: _____

_____

How can I work using more of my strengths? _____

_____

Unleash Your Ideas:

Sometimes you can create a career tailored just for you. It is possible to combine two different careers and interests. For example, a career as a physical therapist utilizes your interests in both healthcare and sports. When you focus your strengths and weaknesses with a realistic and doable strategy, you can make some serious gains. It's about being positive, hardworking, and focused.

THE POWER OF CHOICE

Write down three possible career or job titles that you are considering:

#1 _____

#2_____

#3 _____

Next, score each choice by importance to you:

#1 is most important, #2 is next important, and #3 is the least important.

	Job 1	Job 2	Job 3
Enjoy nature of the work	____	____	____
Enjoy the working conditions	____	____	____
Have the necessary strengths	____	____	____
Want to learn more skills	____	____	____
Fits your personality	____	____	____
The industry is expected to grow	____	____	____
The training/education time is OK	____	____	____
The starting income is acceptable	____	____	____
The career matches my work values	____	____	____
The work matches my personal values	____	____	____
	Choice 1	**Choice 2**	**Choice 3**
Total the points in each column:	#1 ____	# 2 ____	#3 ____

Your choices make a big difference in how your dreams will turn into reality. Your top career choices should be your starting point to do some research. Take these steps by going to Onet.org to learn more about what is required and gain more information.

The careers that I am considering are: _____

and _____

The skills needed are: _____

_____

Check out CareerOneStop.org to find the nearest location. Set up a meeting to discuss your choices. Be prepared with a notebook and questions to get the most out out of each meeting. Try to talk to people who work in that field and can give you more information.

When you are ready to move ahead, consider the following to decide on your chosen career.

If you could start over, what career would you choose? _____

What have you been doing the last few years? _____

_____

What was that like? _____

_____

Where else can you use your skills? _____

_____

How do you feel about going in a different direction? _____

_____

Benefits of making a change: _____

_____

What does success look like for you? _____

_____

NOTES:

7

WORK-RELATED TRAINING AND EDUCATION

IN THE LAST CHAPTER, you narrowed down your career options. In chapter seven you will learn how to strengthen your skills and create a foundation for a better future.

Consider Available Work-Based Programs Including:

1. Training Programs

2. Apprenticeships

3. Community Colleges and 4-Year Programs

4. Private Career Schools

5. Online Education

Developing skills helps you earn more money. Education makes you more productive and valuable to a company. You can never lose your education. When you earn more, you help yourself and the economy. Companies grow and might hire more workers. This can help everyone. The focus needs to be on finding the information about where the opportunities are and what is required. Don't wait for training and a job to come to you. Reach for it. Give yourself a chance to get ahead, begin a successful career and earn more than a living wage.

In most cases plain old fear stops us from trying new things. We're afraid of, "What if I don't like it?" Or, "Should I spend the time and money?" Those challenges can shrink once you commit to trying. Learning new skills will help you discover surprising things about yourself. It keeps your brain sharp, and the process helps you gain confidence.

The story of **Eddie** is an inspiration.[1] To say that Eddie had a tough home life is an understatement. As he grew older, his life at home became more dangerous. A neighbor took him in and gave him stability. Some of the kids he grew up with are still on the streets. Their lives are out of control due to alcohol and drugs. One day, Eddie got a break. One of his former teachers saw Eddie and asked him to meet for coffee. She guided and encouraged him to continue his education. He grew more confident and learned that he was smarter than he thought. It has not been easy. He had to stop taking classes until he earned enough money to pay for his tuition. He decided to work nights and pay for one course at a time.

Both his neighbor and his former teacher were his mentors and helped him realize what he is capable of doing. That tough attitude in school was his coat of armor to protect himself. He came to accept that he could not forget his past but he did not have to let those things control him now. He is learning to manage his feelings and to "get that chip off his shoulder." He has come a long way and feels that he has a bright future. He graduated in December 2016 with a degree in English.

Don't wait to be discovered. This is your chance for you to be the discoverer. Training and education give you the confidence to do well. Find out what resources are out there. When you change your mind, you change your direction. There are free or low-cost job training sites that can not only teach new skills but also sharpen the skills you already have. If you need assistance, your local library can help you find the information. Following is an non-inclusive list of job training sites. There are many more than listed here.

Job Training Resources:

The following nonprofit sites offer short term job training with opportunities for steady work. Many of these training opportunities are free or available at minimal cost. Search for nonprofit training in a city near you.

The Job Training Alliance (JTA.org) is a group of organizations offering training for employment opportunities. On their website, click on "Find a Training Program." The list of training programs include: culinary arts, energy efficient maintenance skills, early education, health care, information technology (IT) and more.

Goodwill.org/Find-Jobs-and-Services offers job training and work opportunity programs. Click on: Find jobs and services or Get Training. You can also call 800-Goodwill to find a center near you.

Platform to Employment (PlatformToEmployment.com) is a nationally recognized program that offers job search assistance and interviewing skills. Their website offers a five-week preparatory program. Upon completion, they help participants find open positions at local companies. They are based in Connecticut and have locations in Cincinnati, Ohio; Chicago, Illinois; Dallas, Texas; Denver, Colorado; Detroit, Michigan; Minneapolis, Minnesota; Newark, New Jersey; San Diego, California; San Francisco, California and Tampa, Florida. They also offer a self-paced, online course.

Year Up (YearUp.org) has locations in Providence, Rhode Island; Boston, Massachusetts; Dallas/Ft. Worth, Texas; Wilmington, Delaware and Los Angeles, California. They provide training in technical careers, customer service and office support for those 18 to 24 years old who meet low income eligibility requirements. "The students spend six months in the classroom learning the skills employers need, then they intern for six months while applying their skills and earning a salary."

Job Corps has 125 locations in the U.S. (Their website is: JobCorps.gov) They connect skills and education for those between 16 and 24 years of age to careers in advanced auto diesel training, network cable installation and office administration.

YMCA Training Inc (YMCABoston.org/traininginc) offers a 20-week computerized office skills training and employment program. Participants can specialize in customer service, financial services, health insurance or medical office support. Call: (617) 542-1800 to apply.

The Salvation Army in Georgia (SalvationArmy.org/Augusta) offers a three-month, tuition-free, women's skills training program. Check out SalvationArmyUSA.org for the counseling and employment programs in their other locations.

Strive International (StriveInternational.org) offers skills training in: green construction, office operations, certified nursing, computer technology, and others. Training goes from four weeks to four months and is free. Click on Strive Affiliate Networks to find their locations in the U.S.

Career Collaborative (CareerCollaborative.org) helps adults 22 to 55 years old with job readiness and career development in the greater Boston area.

TECHNICAL JOB TRAINING

IT (information technology) is a growing field. In many locations, there are three to ten job openings for every IT graduate. Here are some training programs to consider:

Yes We Code (YesWeCode.org) is a private computer training program created by Van Jones with locations in Oakland, California; San Francisco, California; New York, New York; Chicago, Illinois and New Orleans, Louisiana. They teach coding for careers in information technology. Coding is writing instructions for the computer to follow.

Creating IT Futures (CreatingITFutures.org) is a job training program to train women and minorities in preparing and securing information technology (IT) jobs. Their website has information on how to apply. When accepted, you must be able to do eight weeks unpaid training, plus six months of paid, on-the-job training at an employer's location. Check their website for locations in the US.

PerScholas (PerScholas.org) is a non-profit organization that provides tuition-free technology training in computer and networking skills to unemployed or underemployed adults. Check their website for locations in the US. A woman completed their "Women in Technology" program and then got an apprenticeship job.[2] She said that "I now have more than just a job. I am on a career path offering a shot at progress."

Healthcare Opportunities:

Healthcare skills are always in demand. There are many different opportunities from laboratory work and medical records to working with patients in doctor's offices, hospital clinics, recovery centers, and other facilities. You will feel needed and make a difference in people's lives. There are many choices. Contact training sites, schools and colleges for more information.

EMTs (emergency medical technicians) are also in demand. These people drive ambulances and save lives. The projected job growth for EMTs in the next ten years is 24%. Training could be from three to eleven weeks and could take from 30 to 350 hours, depending on where you get your training. If you are interested, search for EMT training classes in your location or search online for EMT Training + your city.

The stories of Jane, Charles and Pat illustrate some of the opportunities.

> **Jane** took a course to become a medical assistant, a job in demand. After several months of applying to local hospitals, she was offered a job. A year and a half later, she was asked if she would be interested in an on-the-job training program to be a Bone Densitometry Technician. She completed the training on how to use the x-ray machine for bone density testing. She studied and received her CBDT (certified bone density technician license). She is now earning a good salary plus health benefits.

> **Charles** worked in a restaurant, then in several office jobs, but was not happy. One day, he learned about the work of a phlebotomist, one who draws blood from patients. Training can be completed in about sixteen weeks. These jobs are always in demand in laboratories, hospitals, doctor offices and nursing homes. He feels that it is a good fit for him and wants to become a supervisor.

> **Pat** enrolled at a technical school to become a medical assistant. A few months into her coursework, she realized that she'd made a mistake. She hated drawing blood. She set up an appointment with her advisor and then transferred into that school's dental assistant program. She was much happier, graduated with honors, and got a good position with benefits.

HIGH SCHOOL EQUIVALENCY TEST:

If you do not have a high school diploma it is never too late to earn your GED (General Education Diploma) or HiSET (High School Equivalency Test). They are equivalent, but the name varies by state. To get your diploma, go to your nearest adult learning center or CareerOne Stop.org for preparation materials for the test. You can also call your state's Department of Education for more information.

Susan worked in a hospital kitchen cleaning trays. She worked hard but saw no future. She was a 43-year-old high school drop-out trying to support her two kids. Her supervisor noticed her strong work ethic and encouraged her to get her high school equivalency diploma. She took evening classes at her public high school. When she completed her education, she went into the hospital training program to be a unit clerk. She is learning skills at work, earning a better salary and has more opportunity. One adult graduate said, "There is nothing second-hand about a high school equivalency diploma."[3]

APPRENTICESHIP PROGRAMS:

These run two to four years on average. They offer a good future, once you complete the training. These programs are sometimes hard to get into. The majority of apprenticeships are in building and manufacturing trades. However, a healthcare company recently took on IT (information technology) and project management apprenticeships.

Where can you find apprenticeship programs? Check out CareerOneStop.org/toolkit/apprenticeships. You can also look up Apprenticeships.gov. Not all apprenticeships are union-based. Registered apprenticeships include unions but are also offered at community colleges, workforce investment boards in many states, industry associations and private companies. Most apprenticeships include both on-the-job training and classroom instruction provided by training centers. Apprenticeships can cover many occupations including carpentry, child care development specialist, construction craft laborer, elevator construction, fire medic, industrial machine mechanics, law enforcement agent, locksmith, pipe fitter, information technology specialist and many more.

Companies often have a hard time finding candidates with the right skills. Some companies are starting their own apprenticeship programs that combine classroom and on-the-job training with pay. IBM wants candidates with a high school education or equivalency and some familiarity with coding but does not require any certifications or technical job experience.[4] At this writing, there are several hundred openings at their locations in Massachusetts, North Carolina, Texas and California. Carousel Industries, located in Rhode Island, focuses on communications and data networks. The company is also starting its own apprenticeship program.

Building Pathways:

BuildingPathwaysBoston.org is a six-week program in Boston and also in Worcester, Massachusetts that introduces people to careers in the building trades, followed by a guaranteed placement into an apprenticeship program. It is an intensive program that combines classroom instruction with hands-on training and a strong amount of career readiness skills. Thus far, over 100 graduates have been placed in 17 trades.

Corey bounced between jobs. Nothing seemed to be a good fit for this energetic guy.[5] He heard about a partnership between Waste Management Co., Civicorps, and unions that gives high school dropouts an opportunity to become Teamster drivers after completing their training. After two years, they are eligible for union jobs and then will be working toward a pension. Through Civicorps he was accepted into their truck driver training program and is now able to support his family. Corey said, "I couldn't get there myself. I am thankful for this opportunity through Civicorps."

Job ladders refer to a progression from entry-level to high level jobs. You can start at any level when you have the education required for that position. The higher paying jobs are at the top of the career ladder.

Healthcare Occupations:

Physician   (DR)

Physician's Assistant   (PA)

Registered Nurse   (RN)

Licensed Practical Nurse   (LPN)

Certified Nursing Assistant (CNA)

Home Health Aide

These are only some examples of the many opportunities in the healthcare field.

Construction: In the building trades, career opportunities might include:

Construction foreman

Tile or brick setter

Stone mason

Carpenters

Machine operators and others.

At this time, there is a great shortage of skilled laborers.[6] The hardest jobs to fill include electricians, carpenters, welders, bricklayers, plasterers, plumbers, masons and more. Many workers in the skilled trades earn average to above average wages. Salaries depend on which field you work in. According to the Bureau of Labor Statistics, in 2018 the median wage is $43,600 for carpenters and $52,000 for electricians. There is a need for more workers to meet the demand.

COMMUNITY COLLEGES AND FOUR-YEAR COLLEGE PROGRAMS:

Some older students hesitate to return to a classroom. They might have other responsibilities that make scheduling a challenge. Sometimes you have to recreate yourself in a different area to get ahead. There is no age limit to going to school. You have the option to take one accredited course at a time. This way, you pay the tuition as you go.

Make an appointment with the financial aid department of the school you are considering to discuss your options. Do your homework. Start by finding out what the demand is for the career you are interested in. Ask what skill level you will be at when completing the program and what the demand is to hire graduates in your area. Does the school have a good reputation? Do the instructors work in the industry they are focused on? Many of the schools offer placement services after completion of the certificate or degree program.

There are several ways to learn about certification requirements for different jobs. You can go to CareerOneStop.org to look up jobs by keyword, by lists of industries and by occupations that require certifications. They also hold career boot camps to prepare you for your job search.

For more information, contact your state's department of higher education, then click on the office of certification. You will find which fields require certifications, the average length of time to get certified, and the average salary earned after certification.

Community colleges offer many career options. A strong area for career opportunities is in STEM (Science, Technology, Engineering and Math). Jobs requiring an Associate Degree include laboratory technician, advanced manufacturing and others. Many of their courses can prepare you for certification in various fields. For example, a community college program can prepare you for the FAA (Federal Aviation Administration) certification in aviation maintenance. These jobs are in demand and pay well. There are certification programs in fiber optics, computer science, construction technology, healthcare, paralegal and many more. Please look at the catalog of courses at the schools you are interested in.

Many community colleges offer skills assessments to help identify your academic strengths and weaknesses. They offer assistance in selecting your study track and may have tutors to help with the classwork. Many of these services are free. They also offer college credit for life experiences such as military training, prior work experience, employment training and other situations. Many schools have mentoring programs to help you navigate working part-time and completing your coursework on time. Ask the counseling office if a mentoring program is available at the school you are considering. The mentoring is free and can be very helpful.

If you are applying to college and have a high school equivalency diploma, you can overcome any disadvantage with examples of projects completed, evidence of work experience and references. You can start at a two-year college. When you graduate, you will have proven to be as prepared as any other high school graduate. If you applied and were not accepted, send a letter to the head of the admissions department stating that you have changed your behavior. Explain how you have become more mature and now understand the value of an education. State your goals and what you want to accomplish. Tell them how motivated you are and ask for a second chance.

FINANCIAL AID:

The school's financial aid office will help you to explore options for grants and scholarships to help pay tuition, such as:

1. The Federal Aid Pell Grant,
2. The Federal Supplemental Educational Opportunity Grant and
3. The Federal Work Study Program.

Contact the school that you are considering for more information. Go to the website FAFSA.ed.gov and fill out a FAFSA form. This is a free application for federal student aid. See if you are eligible based on financial need.

Consider working full-time and taking one course each semester in the evening to manage tuition expenses. If you are in school less than half-time, you probably won't be eligible for federal or private student loans. However, if you pay as you go (paying for one course at a time), you won't be left with a huge loan to repay over many years' time. Granted, it will take longer to complete your studies but it is better than graduating with a large debt.

You can look for scholarships at CareerOneStop/find scholarships, College Scholarships.com, myscholly.com or Scholarships.com. Instead, print out the application and mail it to the appropriate person and address found on their website.

Private Career Schools:

Many students have spent a lot of money on tuition at a private career school and later found out that their course work either did not qualify them to get the job they trained for or their school was about to be closed by the state for false advertising. These students were left with large student loans and no jobs. To prevent this from happening to you, take the time to contact your state's Attorney General's Department of Higher Education to ask about the school you are considering before spending any money on tuition. You want to know if the school has ever been placed on probationary status for failure to bring their programs into compliance with the Department of Education's requirements. Ask if the school is accredited. Unaccredited schools are not eligible for federal student loans. Choose a not-for-profit school in your state that is accredited by your state's board of education. This means their programs meet the standards of the board of education in that state.

In researching schools, ask to sit in on a class. Are the facilities and equipment the same as described in their literature? Get the facts on financial aid, grant or loans and work-study programs. Know how and when the funds are dispersed and how the loans are repaid. Your best option is to look at a public community college that offers many vocational training choices at reasonable costs. Set up an appointment with a counselor at the school you are interested in.

ONLINE EDUCATION:

Did you know that you can get a good education, at your own pace, online? Don't have a computer? Most public libraries have computers that you can use, free of charge. The librarian is there to answer occasional questions. The advantages of on-line schools are that you can:

a) Stay at home (no commute),

b) Study and take one course at a time,

c) Pick your own schedule and,

d) Choose subjects that you are interested in.

For those over fifty years old, you can choose from many free college courses. Look at the Lifelong Learning Programs at your state's department on aging or on OsherFoundation.org. There are hundreds of courses. Check to see if the courses you are interested in offer college credits that might be applied to a degree program.

Free Online Classes:

There are thousands of educational courses online to expand your knowledge. One is called MOOC.list.com which stands for Massive Open Online Courses that are free but do not earn college credits. Some schools offer MOOC courses for a fee. The course can give you information to help decide if you want to learn more about that subject. It could be a stepping stone to a new career.

Edx.org offers free online classes from many colleges and universities world-wide.

You could earn a certificate in the area you are interested in. Some, but not all, classes are credit-eligible. Be sure and check out if the course you want will offer college credits. UniversalClass.com is also free on your computer. All you need is a library card. These courses do not offer college credit. A librarian can show you how to sign up. There are over 500 courses, ranging from accounting and web development to cake decorating. You have six months to complete each class. These classes are self-paced and are led by certified instructors available online to answer your questions.

Free Clemente Courses:

Many free Clemente Courses (ClementeCourse.org) are given across the United States.[7] On their website, click on *Course Directory* to find a location near you. These free courses expose people to instruction in the humanities and help people learn that there is more to life. Students meet twice a week for two semesters and take courses in moral philosophy, literature, art history, American history and writing. The admission requirements are: that the student's family gets by on less than what is considered a living wage and that the student cannot have graduated from college. Earl Shorris, the founder of Clemente Courses, said that many poor people are so involved in daily struggles that there is no time for them to grow.

Their website offers motivating stories of successful students. "Courses change people's lives. It helps them think better," said Waldo, one of their students. He dropped out of high school, got his GED, and started the Clemente courses given at his local health center. He carried over his six credits to Roxbury Community College in Massachusetts. From there, he enrolled at Suffolk University. He is on track to graduate with a degree in Applied Legal Studies. He said, "I never even knew what college credits were. Look at me now."

TIPS FOR DOING WELL IN CLASS:

Never miss a class. Plan to study every day. Make it a priority. Write the time that you will study on your calendar. Write in your calendar when the assignments and tests are due. If you see it, you will do it. Be friendly with classmates who are good students. They could be positive role models and good influences. Be open to feedback. Ask questions when you are unsure. Learn to focus and say no to distractions. Your education and your future come first. Be aware of your thoughts and your daily routine.

If you are overwhelmed, take one course at a time. Schools offer tutoring and study labs. Don't hesitate to ask for help. It shows that you care enough about yourself to do well. If you took a test and didn't get the grade you wanted, you could say, "I still have the ability to do well. Next time, I will start studying earlier so I can review the work before the test. I see what my mistake is. I will fix it and learn from it."

Regina dropped out of high school, had a child and worked in the fast food industry. There wasn't enough money to make ends meet. Her drive to take care of her child kicked in. She studied at night and earned her high school equivalency diploma. She got a job as a hairdresser and worked part-time. She learned of a career workshop for women, enrolled at a community college, got an internship, and then found a job as a process technician. She doesn't have to work two jobs now and has health insurance for herself and her son. She said, "Determination doesn't pay the bills, but it makes getting to the bank a little easier."[8]

WORK-RELATED
TRAINING AND EDUCATION

My idea of what I want to do: _____

_____

When: _____

Where:_____

My training plan is: _____

_____

_____

The schools or training institutions I will contact for more information are: _____

_____

_____

Prerequisites for admission: _____

_____

Costs: _____

_____

Lengths of time to complete the program: _____

_____

Certifications required for the job I want to do: _____

_____

The requirements to get that certification are: _____

_____

My questions are: _____

_____

The skills I need to learn are: _____

_____

Salary expected the first year at the job: _____

Is this reasonable for me? _____

My financial requirements:

Medical: _____

Rent: _____

Utilities:_____

Food: _____

Transportation: _____

Other: _____

Time frame: _____

My questions are:_____

_____

NOTES:

8

DEALING WITH OBSTACLES

IN THE LAST CHAPTER, we discussed options for training and education. Chapter 8 is filled with tips and suggestions to overcome obstacles and keep your eye on the prize: a better future.

Getting out of your comfort zone is scary. It is easier not to go into unfamiliar territory. Give yourself a chance. Be aware of what you are thinking and feeling. Be honest with yourself. Why is this important? What will my life be like when I achieve my goals? You only get what you ask for. Be bold and say, "I am worth it." Do not underestimate yourself. You will be stronger for it.

Here's the thing: when things don't go as planned, focus first on having an optimistic attitude. Then do what needs to be done. Preparation for your job search is the key to reaching your goals. It puts you in control. You will feel more confident and motivated when you have a plan.

Start by acknowledging that the process of getting a job or changing direction is stressful. A natural impulse is not to ask for help. The truth is, everyone needs help at some time. Accepting support from your mentor and others is better than OK.

YOU'VE GOT THREE CHOICES IN LIFE -

GIVE UP,

GIVE IN OR

GIVE IT ALL YOU'VE GOT!

– Charleston Parker

Make a Good First Impression:

Work on "first impressions." When you are getting ready to look for a job, it is important that you look professional. Appearance is important because it shows that you care about yourself. Check out these organizations:

Dress for Success provides women's work-appropriate outfits, free of charge. Call for more information. The website lists their locations: DressForSuccess.org

Career Gear provides men's clothing free of charge. They also offer life skills and job readiness programs. They serve men via referral agency approved appointments only. Go to CareerGear.org to find their locations.

Be aware of how you come across. People who are generally likable have a friendly attitude. They are not moody or quick to judge. They smile. They usually nod to signal that they are listening. They don't interrupt. They ask good follow-up questions. Don't underestimate the importance of your attitude.

Emotional Intelligence:

Daniel Goleman, the author of *Working with Emotional Intelligence*, said, "It doesn't matter how smart the candidate is but how well he or she relates to other people."[1] People with low emotional intelligence may not be sure about how they appear to others. The good news is that emotional intelligence can be learned. The most accurate predictor of success in your personal life and at work is your emotional intelligence. It is the ability to understand and apply that knowledge to various situations. People who seem more effective are those who appear to be approachable and cooperative. They are willing to share information without anticipating something back in return. They are more aware of how they are perceived by others. They come across as being open to suggestions and have learned how to control their emotions. They can swallow their pride and admit their mistakes. Most importantly, they acknowledge when others do well.

Emotional intelligence is critical in an interview. This is why: a company has two candidates for the same job. One is well-qualified but a little arrogant. When asked why he left his last job, he blamed his former boss. The second candidate did not have as much experience as the first guy. However, he came across as easy-going, accepted direction and stayed focused. That is why he was offered the job. A company can train a worker in technical skills. It's harder to deal with someone who does not take criticism easily and is hard to get along with. Interviewers are aware of emotional intelligence.

Emotional intelligence helps us understand not only ourselves but also what makes others tick. Emotional intelligence does not have to do with how smart you are. It is about using your people skills so others feel that you are interested, are listening and care about what they are saying. Your skills to do a job are important. A large part of getting ahead is that you can fit in with the employees at the company you are applying to. That is why emotional intelligence is so important. The five parts of emotional intelligence are:

1. Being aware of what we say and do;

2. Using our self-control by staying calm under stressful situations;

3. Showing that we are motivated by our commitment and optimism;

4. Understanding others and;

5. Using good social and communication skills.

Get Help From Your Mentor:

By having your mentor help you make a more positive impression, you will come across as a stronger candidate. Know what you have to offer. Speak about your accomplishments with confidence.

Face up to your mistakes and what you learned so that those mistakes will not be repeated. A temporary setback is a motivator to keep at it. It is not an excuse to give up. There is no such thing as 100% success. Everyone has gone through hurdles. Anything worth doing comes with some bumps in the road. It's time to be honest. Are you using your past problems as an excuse to stop trying? Picture yourself with a better outcome. Wishing doesn't make it happen. Growth requires change. Learn to respond to various situations more confidently. Do not let the fear of making a change destroy your chances of getting a good job. If you are turned down, it might just inspire you to work a little harder on your job search. Nothing inspires more determination than seeing the light at the end of the tunnel.

Athletes use a mind-training method called "imagery" or mental rehearsals to fix mistakes before they happen.[2] It is better to be prepared in advance instead of being surprised by questions that you did not expect. You are going into an interview. Know what the company's business is. Prepare questions in advance to ask the interviewer at the end of the meeting. Practice acting with confidence. Be approachable and interested. Have two or three rehearsed sentences ready when asked "Tell me about yourself." No matter what the outcome of that meeting is, go over your script and repair any problems before your next interview.

Say you didn't get that job. Your temper rises. Be aware of how you are reacting and how long it takes you to calm down. If you feel doubt and anxiety, it is usually caused by fear. We worry "what if?" Be aware of what triggers you. The closer we look at what we are thinking, the more we might realize that those thoughts may not be true at all. Our feelings can drive our fears.

> ✎ *Gain control of your emotions by using these helpful tension reducing tools to get back in control:*
>
> **Play calming music**
>
> **Go for a walk or do exercises**
>
> **Practice gratitude for the little things you appreciate**
>
> **Keep a diary or a notebook**
>
> **Get enough sleep**
>
> **Meet regularly with your mentor**
>
> **Use mindfulness to help manage your thoughts**

It's important to understand what to do so it doesn't happen again. It makes the difference between behaving out-of-line or behaving in an acceptable way. You have more to gain when you are calm and focused.

Rejection is part of the process of getting a job. It happens to most people. Keep the rejection in perspective. Avoid putting all your hopes into one job application. Instead of saying, "I'll be devastated if it doesn't work out," say, "If this one doesn't work out, there are more jobs that I am qualified to do." Make a commitment to yourself to apply for other opportunities. Rejection teaches us what works and what does not. It teaches us to change so we do not make the same mistakes again. We learn by trial and error.

Accept that you are not a victim. Instead of avoiding things that make you uncomfortable, find the strength to work for a better future. Take responsibility. We always have choices. Someone who is a perfectionist might say, "I am successful if I get the job." Life is not rigid like that. If you accept your feelings and focus on your skills, it will be easier to move forward in a more productive way.

APPLY WHAT YOU'VE LEARNED:

The difference between feeling defeated or getting up and moving on is how you apply what you have learned to help manage your emotions. As you feel better about who you are, you will think of other choices. If plan A does not work out, develop a back-up plan. Believe in your own strengths. See your problems as challenges to overcome. Getting a job is not only about how deserving you are. It is also about how much effort you put in. Your motivation sets an example for you and your family.

> **Kari** had a bad work history. Something always happened that made her leave her job. Yet, she had good skills. One day, she was told of a job opportunity. She followed up and got an interview. When she was questioned about her work history, she stumbled. Kari did not answer the questions directly. Instead, she asked the hiring manager about the salary and benefits. It appeared either that she was trying to avoid her job history or that she was more interested in what she would get out of the company rather that what she could bring to the job. She made the mistake of not answering in a way that would meet the company's needs. Later, she spoke with her mentor and said, "I need to learn how to present myself better. I didn't feel confident because I wasn't prepared for the interview. I looked down, appeared uncomfortable and did not answer the questions clearly. Next time, I will be better informed about what the company does, the job requirements and what I can bring to the job."

Realistic flexibility is needed to do well and reach your goals. If jobs in a nearby area are not available, would you be willing to travel further to work? Remember, a few new behaviors can make a big change. Develop the skills and confidence to rise above setbacks. If your goals are unrealistic or not a good fit, you might not get the results you want. If your goals are laid out in small steps, you will gain the strength and traction to go forward.

Your job is to come to the job interview prepared and ready to answer the tough questions. Your responses to the interviewer's questions can make or break an opportunity. When you have prepared answers to some tough questions, you won't be taken off-guard.

People are let go for a variety of reasons. How to handle it? Be sure to have a story that demonstrates that the situation has been dealt with and is no longer an issue. Pay attention to see if any of these situations apply to you:

I was fired: "I was fired at XYZ Construction Company because I was late a lot." The real reason that I was late is that I had difficulties at home. My life fell apart. I did not want to admit my problems. With the help of my mentor, I went into counseling. Since then, I have set goals and have done volunteer work. I now am working part-time and am reliable. I am excited about the opportunity here and will be a dependable and trust-worthy employee."

I was arrested: Handle this by admitting your mistakes. You could say that you made some bad decisions. Write out your story before the interview and practice. You want to give a convincing story with true examples of what you learned and how you corrected your past behavior. CareerOneStop.org has an entire section (Ex-Offenders) on its website filled with good suggestions.

The job search has taken a long time: A red flag on an application form or a resume is that you have been out of work for a long time. These gaps need to be explained in a positive light. You might say that you used that time to do volunteer work or to learn new skills. It would be good if the volunteer work or training that you did is related to the skills needed at the job you are applying for.

Why did you leave your last job? Have a prepared answer. If you and your former employer agreed that it was a mutual separation, you could say that there was a re-organization in the company and your position changed. You are looking for a growth opportunity with more responsibility. You will devote your time and energy to (job title). Stay positive. Do not bad mouth your old boss or former workers.

Did not finish school: I have matured and now have the desire to finish what I start.

Little Experience: I learn quickly. I will work hard. I am reliable.

Physical Limitation or Disability: Explain why your disability or limitation won't interfere with your performance on the job. Do not be defensive. Just explain the facts. The employer wants to know that you can handle the duties of the job.

The American Disabilities Act works to prevent discrimination against people with disabilities. It means that if an employee or potential employee is capable of performing a task, he or she should not be treated differently than any other person who is also capable of performing that task.

Aren't you overqualified for the job? Your prepared answer might be "Because of my skills and experience, I could start with no down-time for training. I am in good health, dependable and ready to work. I will be an asset to your company." Give examples of your achievements to demonstrate that you can do the job. Reframe the situation: "I am learning something new each time."

The U.S. Equal Employment Opportunity Act enforces federal laws prohibiting workplace discrimination based on race, color, national origin, sex and religion.

The Age Discrimination in Employment Act prohibits discrimination against persons 40 years or older. If an applicant is asked a question based on any of these topics, bring the conversation back to the job you are applying for and the skills needed for the position. If you are worried about age discrimination, you can leave off school attendance or career training dates. You can show the list of 15-20 years of employment history. You do not have to list every job you had.

There are transition counseling and senior employment centers in every state that help mid-life job seekers. AARP.org has a program that matches senior employment programs with local non-profits for those over 55 years old. Job seekers 45 and older in Massachusetts and New Hampshire can contact OperationAble.net for assistance. They suggest that people look at newer and smaller companies in their job search. Be aware of your attitude. There is sometimes a fear that an older worker will be a "know-it-all" or bossy. You want to appear friendly and professional.

If you are overwhelmed and feel that too much is on your plate, talk it over with your mentor and/or a counselor.

IT'S NOT HOW MANY TIMES YOU WERE KNOCKED DOWN, BUT
HOW MANY TIMES YOU GOT UP.

- Rocky Marciano, world champion prizefighter

DEALING WITH OBSTACLES

Remind yourself that you are worth it. Recognize your strengths and talents. Name three that you want to improve: _____

_____

What problems are you working on? _____

_____

What are your options? _____

_____

What are the pros and cons of each choice?

Option 1 _____

_____

_____

Option 2_____

What additional information do I need? _____

_____

_____

My questions are:_____

_____

_____

_____

NOTES:

9

Job Search Strategies

"Your work is going to fill a large part of your life, and the only way to be truly satisfied is to do what you believe is great work. If you haven't found it, you keep looking. Don't settle. Your time is limited, so don't waste it living someone else's life. And most important, have the courage to follow your heart and intuition. As with all matters of the heart, you'll know when you find it."

- Steve Jobs, Apple Co-Founder

THE INFORMATION ON JOB search will give you a head start to not only gain employment, but also to find your way to a career.

You want to identify the companies in your commuting area that would hire someone with your skills. With that said, don't bypass small companies as potential employers. Eighty percent of the companies in the United States are small firms. Do some searching to identify companies that would hire people who do the job that you want to do. Think about this: many jobs are never advertised.

Helpful Job Sites:

The following sites let you identify companies by industry, by job title or by city. Check out the local chamber of commerce in each city you would be willing to work in. You can also go to the Better Business Bureau (BBB.org) and check for facts about that firm. Another resource is the internet where you can identify companies by category (such as electricians). There are many Career One Stop centers (CareerOneStop.org) located in the state you live in. Type in your zip code to find a center near you. There are job openings posted online. There you can get free advice, job leads and job search workshops. The time doing the digging for potential opportunities is well-spent. The information you find will tell you what each company specializes in and gives you further information to use when you go for that interview. You want to match your skills to what the company needs. Many larger companies list their job openings on their web site. Click on "careers" at the top of the home page to see their job openings and their job requirements.

Other job leads can be found online at Indeed.com, SimplyHired.com, CareerBuilder.com, Monster.com and many more. These sites let you search by job title, location and skill level. Use these sites to locate your target companies and learn about any job openings and the qualifications the firm is looking for. There are many websites for specific careers such as medical or construction. Just type in the name of the job + job openings.

Uncover Job Leads:

Informational interviews are another way to get job leads and referrals for job opportunities. You are not being interviewed for a specific job at this time. You want to get information about the career you are interested in. Call the receptionist for the name of the manager of the department that you are interested in. When handled well, it could lead to a possible job interview.

Potential employers want to know specifics of what you did and what problems you solved. Vague language does not demonstrate good communication skills. They want to know the types of projects you worked on, what was accomplished and the results. Give examples of how your skills would help the company that you are interviewing with.

It is important to learn more about the company that you will be speaking with. What are their divisions? What products or services do they specialize in? Type in the company name + manager of the _____ department on a computer at home or in a library. It helps your confidence when you do your homework and feel prepared.

Write down a few sentences telling about what you are looking for and why you are qualified. When you rehearse it, the words should flow naturally and smoothly. A sample script might go like this, "Good morning (or afternoon). My name is _____. I am calling to see if we could meet for an informational interview at a time that is convenient for you. I am looking for a position as _____ and was told that you could help me learn more about that type of work and locate job opportunities in this area. My background includes: offer 2 or 3 sentences about your skills and accomplishments as a (job title) _____." Have a notebook to write down any leads and helpful information.

At the informational interview, dress professionally. Stand straight and walk in with confidence. Come prepared. Bring a resume or application sheet listing your skills and experience. When someone says, "What do you do?" You might answer, "Right now I am looking for work in _____ (type of work) and am interested in what you do at _____ (name of company)." By doing that, you are back in charge of the conversation and might get more information to help direct your search.

Sample questions you might ask at the informational interview are:

1. How did you get into this field?

2. What parts of the job do you really enjoy?

3. What is a typical day on the job like?

4. What skills and experience are most important?

5. What is significant about this company (compared to its competition)?

6. What are the biggest challenges in this industry?

7. Where would you suggest I look for a position?

8. Do you have any advice for me?

9. Is there anyone else that you could refer me to?

The current employees of a company you're interested in working for could be good unofficial recruiters for you. If you know someone or can get a referral from a person who works at that firm, it's a good job lead. Ask if there are any job openings coming up.

Want Ads:

Many want ads do not list specific duties. Some ads are blind, meaning they do not list the company name. For those jobs, put together a sheet that you can use to respond to the ad. Go over a few job descriptions that interest you and then write down your experience to show how it matches the qualifications.

Completing The Job Application:

The application form is a legal document. If you lie about your schooling or anything else, you could be fired. On an application form, be neat. Bring a fact sheet of your work history, including dates, addresses, etc., with you to complete the application form. Spell correctly. Answer each question. This paper is your first impression with the company you are applying to. When asked why you left, use positive phrases such as "left for more responsibility." Answer compensation questions exactly as asked (hourly, weekly or yearly.) Your answer is frequently verified before hiring.

In writing your work history, start with your current or most recent position then list your previous job and so on. State the dates from _____ to _____ by year of your employment. Example: 2007-2014 Lead Machinist, XYZ Company, Hometown, USA.

Have several sentences ready that list your skills and experience. Some examples:

- Fifteen years of manufacturing experience in heavy equipment
- Background in production and in inventory control
- 2015-2018 Operated cranes and trained new operators

Resumes:

Resumes are used to show how your skills and experience relate to the job that you are applying for. There are two types of resumes. One is a chronological resume listing your work experience by date, with the most recent job at the top. The second type is a functional or skills resume that focuses on what you do and emphasizes your strengths. If you had long breaks between jobs or are trying to change into a new field, use the functional resume. Many books at libraries have resume examples. If you are an entry-level candidate, keep your resume to one page. If you have a high school education or higher, include that information plus any training related to the job you are applying for.

Key Words:

You want to use key words that show the hiring manager that you have experience in their industry. Choose from this list of strong action words that match your job skills: Achieved, Approved, Completed, Created, Delivered, Developed, Demonstrated, Doubled, Directed, Eliminated, Expanded, Increased, Improved, Introduced, Performed, Promoted, Purchased, Reorganized, Revised, Scheduled, Serviced, Simplified, Sold, Solved, Started, Succeeded, Supervised, Trained, Tripled, Uncovered, Won and Worked On.

Work Experience:

Include important details about your work experience. What makes you a qualified candidate? How does your experience relate to the job that you are applying for? Include key projects that emphasize your skills to the company. For example, if you worked in construction, focus on,

> a) How did you make money for your past employer? An example might be: brought in #_____ new customers that amounted to $_____ in new sales.

> b) How did you save money for the company? An example might be: finished the job within budget and on time.

> c) How did you make things go smoothly? What problem did you solve? An example of this could be: "reduced production time by ____% over one year's time by implementing a new program_____. For example, in construction, include details of the type and size of the projects you worked on, such as the dollar value, square feet, etc.

> d) Why are you a qualified candidate?

> e) How does your experience relate to the job that you are applying for?

> f) Did you receive praise from your customers? Keep notes of what the customers said about your work performance.

Asking For References:

Select people who would give you positive references. Always ask that person for permission to use his or her name as a reference first. If you cannot list a former employer, go to people who can speak well about your character and your work skills. Keep a list of your references, the names (check spelling) and contact information you used when filling out an application form or in an interview.

FINDING EMPLOYMENT RECRUITERS:

Employment recruiters review candidates' job experiences and place candidates in jobs at their client companies. There is no charge to a candidate. When calling a recruiter, state the type of job you are interested in and the reason that you are qualified. Ask for an opportunity to meet with the recruiter. Treat the meeting as important as a job interview. Refer to chapter 8 on how to answer difficult questions about your background.

Share a story of how you worked well with others and that you pay attention to details. If you have an example of how you solved a work-related problem, blend that into the conversation. Give examples in the conversation, where appropriate, that you are a problem- solver, a hard worker, and have good communication skills.

Here is an example: "Recently I learned that my employer was going to hire outside consultants for a project installation. I had the experience and worked with in-house staff in less time and saved the company $. _____. I would like to work full-time at a company where I can work with a team that focuses on _____ and I can use my skills in _____."

Think like the manager that would hire you. What skills would the company want for this position? Read the job description you are interested in. Be sure and ask the recruiter:

1) What are the main qualifications that your client (the hiring company) is looking for?

2) What is the reason for the job opening?

3) What is the compensation package? (salary + benefits)

4) Where is the job located?

Be prepared. Both the recruiter and the company interviewer want to know why the firm should offer you the job.

Relate your skills to the skills needed for that position. Then fill out this worksheet for the job mentioned in the ad:

Skills Needed   **Your Qualifications**

_____   _____

_____   _____

_____   _____

PREPARING FOR AN INTERVIEW:

You landed an interview. Now, take the time to prepare. Show that you are interested enough to do your homework about the industry, what the company does and the position you are interviewing for. Read the company's job description and focus on the requirements as if you were hiring that person. No one has every requirement listed. Focus on the "must have" skills for that job and fine tune your resume or application to emphasize how you meet those requirements. Think about this. If you were hiring someone for the job you are interviewing for, what skills and qualifications would be important?

There are other interview questions that you might be asked and it would be good to practice your response:

1. Why do you want to work at this company? (That's where company research is useful.)

2. What can you do for us? Use examples from your past experience and connect those experiences to the job you are interviewing for,

3. How will you get along with the other people working there?

4. Why are you an ideal candidate? Use your accomplishment stories.

5. Answer the salary question with a salary range. Do your research online before the interview at Salary.com or PayScale.com.

Tips for successful interviewing: Do not come across as a know-it-all and have your intentions interpreted as arrogance. You can avoid that by not correcting the interviewer and by being a good listener. Listen carefully to the whole question. Wait until the interviewer finishes speaking before you answer. Do not interrupt. Try to understand what he or she is getting at. Restate the question if you are not sure of what is being asked. Take a few seconds to think of how you will answer the question. Show the interviewer that you understand by answering each question directly. Keep calm and give clear answers. Practice with your mentor. It will help to build your confidence.

The night before the interview: Check out the route and how much time you will need to get there. Review your company research and your notes. Have a copy of your application form or resume ready to take with you. Eat well. Get a good night's rest. Stay calm and think positive thoughts.

Before going into the interview: Instead of thinking, "I'll get this over with," think, "I have done my homework. I will listen carefully. I will explain why I am a good fit. I am ready to nail it."

The day of the interview: First impressions count. Before the job interview, be courteous to everyone, the receptionist, etc. Don't look annoyed if you must wait. If you are nervous, try not to show it. Stand straight and walk in with confidence. Smile. Have a firm handshake. Make eye contact. Dress appropriately. Do not smoke or wear clothing that smells of smoke. Don't be so focused on your past history or on future opportunities that you are not in the present. Take a few deep breaths. Remember mindfulness. Breathe slowly to stay calm and focused. Make eye contact but don't stare. Stick to the point. Speak clearly. Avoid sounding defensive and do not give excuses. Never speak negatively about past employers or co-workers. Have a strong story ready about what you can do to meet what the company wants in the winning candidate.

A good way to remember someone's name is to say it out loud. Here is an example:

"Hello, Mr. or Ms. _____. My name is_____.

Focus on your enthusiasm for the job and keep your energy high. Employers want to hire people who want them. Playing "hard to get" or apathetic does not help.

During the interview, it is a good idea to mention how you worked well with your team to solve a problem. Tell your story explaining how your skills would benefit the company you are interviewing with. Here is an example: When asked about a time when something did not go smoothly, how did you solve the problem? Practice your answers before your interviews so you will answer these questions clearly and calmly.

When the interviewer asks: Do you have any questions for me? Be prepared. Focus on the job itself, not the salary. The interviewer is not sold on you yet. Here are examples of questions you might ask the interviewer at the end of the interview:

1. What will be my responsibilities?

2. Who would I report to?

3. What are the most important skills for success on this job?

4 What is your single greatest expectation of the new hire?

5. What do you expect me to do in the first six months?

6. What are my opportunities for growth in this position?

7. What are the next steps in the hiring process?

Thank the interviewer for his or her time. Show interest. Ask when the company will make the hiring decision. Ask for the interviewer's business card so you will have the correct name and address.

THE IMPORTANCE OF NETWORKING:

Networking means connecting with acquaintances and others who can give you referrals of names of department or hiring managers. Employers are more likely to hire people they know or who have been recommended to them. You should be speaking with local store owners, neighbors, former co-workers, classmates, neighbors, coaches or anyone else you can think of to let them know that you are looking for a new position. You have a better chance of gaining an interview from a referral, but there is no guarantee. Always acknowledge your appreciation for his or her help.

Ask your contacts to refer you to some employers that might be hiring. If you say, "I'll take any job," they won't know how to help you. There's a good chance that someone might know of an opening down the road for the work that you want to do. Don't be discouraged by a "no."

Start with a plan and follow it daily. Get organized so you can follow up on any conversations. Track your job search progress. Keep a record of the people you called and any follow-up calls needed. Keep your eye on the finish line. Your end result is to get a job as _____.

Networking events are usually listed in the newspaper under "Calendar." These get-togethers are great places to meet people in your job search. Instead of being overwhelmed, give yourself a goal: make two or three contacts that you can call later. Have an opening line to start a conversation, such as: "What did you think of the speaker?" Prepare a short description about the kind of job you are looking for and your qualifications such as your skills, talents and accomplishments. Practice a few sentences with your mentor. It helps because most people have trouble promoting themselves. You want to be able to say what you have done without bragging. A good way of doing this is tell a work story with accomplishments that apply to the type of work you are looking for.

Close the conversation by saying, "It was great speaking with you. I would love to set up a time to continue our conversation." Remember to get his or her contact information or business card. Write yourself a short note about the conversation to follow-up with later on.

Attending Job Fairs:

A job fair is usually held in a school or other large auditorium. Companies who are looking to fill their open positions set up booths to meet potential candidates. Company literature is available for you to review.

How to stand out at a job fair? The first step is to get a list of the companies that will be there by looking up the job fair online or in a newspaper. That way, you can be prepared to know what the companies do. At the job fair, dress as if you were going to an interview. The first impression is important. Take copies of your application or resume with you. Be able to explain the type of work that you do. You could walk up to the company's booth and say, "Hello. I am looking for a position as a _____ (job title). I read that you have an opening." Hand them a copy of your application or resume with your contact information. Ask for the company representative's business card so that you can follow up. Have a firm handshake and show interest. If you say that you will follow up with a call next week, do so.

Each of your contact records should have the person's name and job title, name of the company, address, phone number and email address, company website and the company's products or services. Also include the date your application or resume was sent, the follow-up date of your phone call, the interview date, a thank you note and the date that you mailed it. Make a note with a follow-up date to check on the status of your application.

Send A Thank You Letter:

Follow up on each interview by sending a thank you letter. The thank you letter acknowledges that you appreciate the time spent at the interview. It's also a good way to keep your name in front of a potential employer.

A Sample Thank You Letter:

Name of Company
Address of Company

Today's date:

Dear _____ ;

Thank you for meeting me on (date) to discuss the position of (job title) at (company name).

You mentioned that you are looking for a person with strong experience in _____.

In my last position, I (list your accomplishments). I also brought in $_____ in new business (or another accomplishment).

Please know that I am very interested in the position and would like to continue our discussions at your convenience.

Sincerely,
(Your signature)

Your name in print

Your address
Your phone number

Be sure and check for correct spelling and grammar.

In your letter, remember to sound interested. Friendly persistence is the key to getting callback from the company. Do not count on only one or two interviews to get a job. Keep your options open by finding networking groups or job clubs listed in the local newspaper. Your local Chamber of Commerce could also help identify business groups. Expand your search to include your new networking contacts.

Call the company you are applying to every few weeks to find out the status of your application. You don't want to pester but you do want them to know that you are interested. Keep a record of when you called, who you spoke with, and the result of the conversation. If they said to call back on a specific date, put that date on your calendar and be sure to follow up.

If you have not had interviews, review the application forms or resume so that your skills and experience are shown in a positive light. If you have not been called back for a second interview, role play with your mentor to help polish your interviewing skills. Choose to have a job that you can look forward to every day. Developing a career plan is necessary. You wouldn't build a house without a blueprint. Your general plan needs details to make it work. Be aware that there are solutions to anticipate setbacks. Stay busy. Do some volunteer work in a field that uses some of the skills needed in the work that you are looking for.

An employment workshop teaches people to anticipate setbacks and rehearse solutions to keep going forward. Locate these workshops at CareerOneStop.org and other job search organizations. (In Massachusetts it is mass.gov/masshire-career-centers.)

A Jobs Program:

A "JOBS" program worth mentioning had remarkable results with its participants. Robert Caplan, co-founder of the JOBS program[1] at the University of Michigan, said that going through the re-employment program helped the participants identify two sets of abilities:

1. Their marketable talents and,
2. Their resiliency to keep trying and learning from each experience.

The more motivated that you are, the better you will learn. This is a prime reason why working with a mentor really increases your chances of reaching your goals. The "JOBS" program was set up in sessions focusing on action learning, interview rehearsals and role playing of stories that demonstrate the applicant's key skills. They were taught to anticipate some downturns. Not every interview will result in a job offer. They learned optimism to keep from fear of failure. They had a support team. A mentor, positive friends or family can help to boost self-confidence and emotional self-control. They learned how to manage their distress and negative emotions so that they can continue to reach their goals. The result was that those participants were re-employed faster than those who did not have that support.

There is an old saying: "Two heads are better than one." The same holds true for job search strategies. It has been shown that using multiple job search strategies and research to find leads in your chosen industry all help move the process forward.

THE PLAN FOR MARKETING YOU

My goals:_____

My priorities:_____

My skills: _____

_____

Market assessment: _____

_____

What is the availability of jobs in the field I have chosen: _____

_____

Is this field growing? The probability of getting a job based on what you learned is: __

_____

My contacts in this field are: _____

_____

_____

_____

_____

_____

Networking sources:

- Job search clubs
- Chamber of Commerce meetings
- Industry Association meetings
- Contacts from my training/education
- Other sources

Sales tools Completed:

- Application form and copies made
- Resumes and copies made
- Cover letter (to answer a job ad)
- Practice my interviewing skills
- Calls made to set up informational interviews
- Tracking my progress and meeting my goals
- Thank you letters written for both informational and job interviews
- Meet regularly with my mentor
- Re-evaluate my strategy as needed

NOTES:

_____
_____
_____
_____
_____

_____
_____
_____
_____
_____
_____

_____

_____
_____

My next meeting is: _____

We will talk about: _____

Questions I will ask at my informational meetings to learn about the field of work that I am interested in:

1. _____

2. _____

3. _____

Questions I will ask at a job interview: _____

_____

My answers to the tough interviewing questions are: _____

_____

A story of my accomplishments: _____

_____

Challenges that I faced: _____

_____

Deadlines that were met: _____

_____

What I accomplished: _____

_____

Results: _____

_____

Questions that I will ask at the end of the interview about the company: _____

_____

_____

Questions that I will ask about the job: _____

_____

_____

_____

_____

_____

_____

NOTES:

10

STARTING A SMALL BUSINESS

BEING YOUR OWN BOSS requires self-discipline. Following your passion is OK but, to be successful you need to have the facts and be laser-focused. This chapter will help you test the waters to see if self-employment is a good idea.

Going in a new direction takes a willingness to learn new skills, make new contacts, and make sure that you have enough income to pay your living expenses. Many dream of having a small business but do not take the time to work out the steps. Begin by putting your idea in writing, then start the preparation. Take the time to discuss this with your mentor.

Being your own boss requires determination. Here is an example. It is snowing out. One teen said, *"My plans are ruined. I can't get to the party."* The other teen said, *"The snow is coming down hard. Let's get our shovels and make some money."* This story shows how two people look at the same situation in two different ways. Be positive and open to opportunity.

When you are thinking about starting a small business, consider your strengths. How comfortable are you at persuasion? Natural salespeople are outgoing and have the drive. Consider your personality. Your skills and personality type are the foundation of the business you are considering. Look at your talents. How do they apply to the business you are considering? Following your passion is good, but to be successful you need to have drive and a detailed plan. A belief in your business is not enough. The hard part is to take the time to work your plan and make it happen.

The Importance of Research:

Do as much research as you can into what it takes to run a business. When you speak to someone with this experience, it will help you avoid some of the hurdles along the way. The Small Business Association (SBA)[1] reported that their clients who received three or more hours of mentoring had higher revenues and increased business growth than those without mentoring help.

One place to start is at your local SCORE office.[2] Score is the nation's largest network of volunteer business mentors. They have over 300 locations in the USA. Their expertise is to help small businesses grow. They help potential start-ups to develop a business plan with advice on finance, marketing and cash flow management. Their free mentoring meetings provide structure and focus. Score also offers a variety of free workshops on many business-related subjects. When something goes wrong, it is good to speak to someone with experience and possibly sidestep any issues before problems arise. Go to: Score.org to find a location near you. On their website, you can search a list of mentors from anywhere in the U.S. who have experience in your type of business. Contact them to set up a phone call at a time that is convenient for you to discuss your business issues. They also take appointments on weekends. These individual mentoring services are also free. Score offices also run a variety of workshops on many business-related subjects.

Have a Business Plan:

Develop a business plan even if you plan to run a small business from home. Understand who your customers are: teens, seniors, veterans, etc. Your sales and marketing efforts need to be focused and spelled out clearly. Project sales and expenses for the business and be realistic when you do so. If you hope to attract alternate funding or investors, whoever you speak with will want to see a carefully constructed plan that outlines the key actions you plan to take and why you believe your idea will succeed. Even if you don't seek funding, writing a business plan helps you think through the steps you need to take, and to set a timetable for accomplishing each objective.

Evaluate What Will Work For You.

Here are some questions you need to consider:

Is there a need and a market for your business? _____

_____

Is the business seasonal? _____

What related experience do you have? _____

_____

What do you like most about this kind of work? _____

_____

Describe your potential customers: _____

_____

Define your customers by category: working families, veterans, teenagers, children,

other: _____

_____

Consider their interests and needs. Why would they buy?_____

_____

What are their needs? _____

How would your product or service meet those needs? _____

_____

Look at your product or service as if you were the customer. Any questions come up?

_____

_____

What is your value to your customers? _____

_____

Who are your competitors? _____

_____

How much competition is there in your area? _____

How would you set yourself apart from your competition? _____

_____

What do your competitors do? _____

Understand your competition and what they offer. What will cause your potential customer to say no? _____

_____

How would you overcome their resistance? _____

_____

What is your competitive advantage for the customer? _____

_____

UNDERSTAND YOUR NUMBERS:

What are your start-up costs? _____

What is the cost of your service or product? _____

What will you charge? _____

Would you charge by the hour or by the job? Would you be able to make a profit and live on that amount? Take your emotions out of your decisions. Look at the reality of whether or not your idea could be successful.

Will that price allow you to make a net profit (after all expenses)? _____

_____

If the numbers do not work, go back and re-work your plan.

How much cash will you need to open your business? _____

Revenue: Where will your revenue come from? _____

Advertising? _____

Direct sales? _____

Other sources? _____

Your break even point is when your revenue or sales covers all your operating costs each month such as a vehicle used for business, insurance, fuel, advertising, raw materials, office supplies, telephone, etc.

What are your break even costs?_____

Suggestion: Take your start-up costs and double them. The number one reason that small businesses fail is that they run out of cash. Where is your income coming from and how will that cash be used?

Cash Flow: Cash flow is so important. How much will you need to run your business weekly or monthly? _____

How much will you need to pay yourself? _____

After you pay yourself, will you still have enough cash to cover your business expenses?

_____

Separate your business and your personal finances. Make sure that you keep your sales tax receipts.

Make a projection with three different results. The first result assumes everything works as you expect. This is your high projection. The second result assumes nothing goes right. The bottom line is not as good as you expected. This is your low projection. The third result assumes steady growth - not fast, not slow. It is based on reasonable expectations. At your third month in business, review these plans and make adjustments to your expenses.

Do some investigating to see if your business idea has a good chance at success. One way is to talk with people who are working in this field (not your direct competitors). Ask good questions: How did you get started? What training did you need? What is necessary to do well? What income would you expect to bring in during the first year? What do you project your income to be later on?

What are your liabilities? Be honest and prepare to avoid problems as much as possible. Pay each month's bills as they become due to avoid paying interest. If it is a seasonal business, plan to put away extra cash for when the business slows down.

If your business sells products, do not over buy supplies or materials before you have orders. You don't want to have a cash flow problem when the bills are due.

If you can work out of your home, establish a budget, line-by-line for phones, vehicle, cost of materials, other business expenses. Control your expenses and adjust your budget to match what your business is bringing in for revenue.

Can you support yourself until you are established? Will you take on part-time work to earn extra income?

A hurdle you might face is that someone might knock down your idea. The people you need to listen to are those who are knowledgeable about your type of business. They are the ones who can give you objective advice and helpful feedback. For those who put your ideas down, set boundaries with friends and family. Are they trying to protect you? Are they envious? Listen to their reasons and criticisms. Don't argue. Be rational. The clear boundaries you set with these folks assure that you stay in control. When you do get together, arguments about your business are "off the table." Listen to your experienced advisors and modify or change direction as needed. Being resilient is showing the ability to bounce back. Create a network with your mentor and advisors to discuss ideas and come up with possible solutions.

CREATE A MARKETING PLAN:

The purpose of a marketing plan is to know what works and what does not. Marketing is about creating an interest in your product or service that becomes a sales lead. Sales mean converting those sales leads into paying customers.

What strategies will you use to grow your customer base?_____

_____

_____

How much will the marketing plan cost? _____

_____

If you want to grow your business by 10%, how much will you have to invest? _____

_____

Look at both new fees and recurring fees to keep the marketing plan moving. Have realistic goals, such as bringing in two new customers a week. Look at your product or service from the eyes of a potential customer.

Do any questions occur to you? How can you answer those questions for a customer?

_____

_____

Advertising Your Business:

Your ad should include a feature. The feature tells what the product or service does. It should also include a benefit. A benefit shows how your product or service can solve a problem. An example might be that it makes their life easier or saves time.

Make your ad copy easy to understand. Keep your budget small by using flyers. Keep the quality good. It reflects how the public will view your business. Your ads should tell how your product or service would solve a problem.

You want to emphasize advantages the customer gets by using your product or service. Marketing raises public awareness of your product or service. Word-of-mouth referrals are critical. You want customers to think that you are the best at what you do.

Co-Market Your Business:

Co-marketing means working with another company that does not compete with you and has similar customers. For instance, a bookstore co-markets with a small food service to share advertising costs. Customers who order get rewarded by getting a small discount in each business. Another example is a landscaping company that advertises its services with a company that paves driveways.

Bundle your services: If your company offers more than one product or service, offer a better price if they order two products or services. Let the customers know that this is a better deal. It is better for you too because it brings in additional income.

Your local Chamber of Commerce is a good place to start to promote your business. Become visible in the community where your business is located. Be social and meet with other business owners to share ideas. Network to increase your list of contacts. Other chamber of commerce members want to get the most out of networking too. Focus on what gets them motivated and you will learn a lot. Be a good listener. Ask: "What can I do for you?" Take notes to remind yourself of names, companies and any important details.

A **couple in Florida** gave each one of their wedding guests a paper mustache on a stick.[3] So many people wanted them that they created a plastic version. They took pictures and put their product on the internet marketplace ETSY.com. They hired someone to develop their website and also put their product on Amazon.com. With more orders coming in, they now have enough income to live on. They started working with a manufacturer to expand their production and are developing new products to keep growing.

If you have a good idea and no cash, don't give up before you start. Use your sweat equity and creativeness. You could buy items from thrift shops and yard sales. Improve the items and then re-sell them. At this point, it is a hobby, not a business. It is a start. Have a plan with a direction and a way of measuring the direction your business is heading. Network and ask others to help get the word out. The local media might run a story about your start-up. Be clear about your costs and your cash flow.

The most important part of your business is the customer. James Stephenson wrote in *Entrepreneur Magazine* that there are twenty-five characteristics of success.[4] Here are a few of them: Do what you enjoy, plan well and focus on selling. He said that *"If everything you do is customer-focused, you are moving in the right direction."*

You have to plan your customer service. Planning means training how you would respond to any situation. A "thank you" goes a long way. If the customer feels ignored, you probably won't get a referral. If they feel valued, they are likely to be repeat customers and refer their friends to you.

Ask the customer, "What can I do for you?" Show interest, smile and don't interrupt. Listen carefully to what the other person is saying. Takes notes, follow through and get back to them as soon as possible. Selling is about finding a need and then filling that need. Have prepared answers ready on how you would handle objections to closing the sale. Is the objection based on the price, product need or timing of the sale? Know what your competitors are offering so you can do better.

Ask for the sale: When the customer says, "I'll think about it," you could reply: "Is there any reason why we can't schedule a delivery by Wednesday?" If they have a good relationship with you, they are more likely to give you their business. Get your customers to try out the product so they can picture themselves using it. It often takes more than one sales call to get the sale. It won't happen unless you ask for their business. When the customer has a good experience, he or she might refer you to other potential customers.

Paul Romano, the owner of several restaurant chains, told his story to *Fortune Magazine* about what it took to grow his business.[5] He stated that, "it takes responsibility to do things right and fix what is not right. Honesty is important.; your reputation will increase by word-of-mouth. Always make people feel appreciated."

Have invoices with you so you can accept payment by check. If you offer credit, spell out in writing your terms (number of days until payment is due), and be sure they are clearly written on the invoice so there is no confusion or ill will. If you offer credit, such as payment in 30 days, be sure your cash on hand is adequate for this. Otherwise, offering a monthly credit plan could create a cash flow problem for you.

For small businesses, insurance companies lump the following coverage into a business or commercial package. General liability covers damages from you or your employees' wrongdoing. Vehicle insurance is necessary. A good insurance broker will evaluate your risks and help you get the coverage you can afford without leaving you liable to costly risks.

When you are ready to add an employee, consider hiring a vet. He or she may have the experience that you need. A vet also offers a strong work ethic and is team-oriented. Employers may be eligible for a Work Opportunity Tax Credit (WOTC) for hiring veterans. Search for more information on doleta.gov/WOTC. There are many good reasons to hire vets. You can read about them at the "Veterans Employment Tool Kit" offered by the U.S. Department of Veteran Affairs. You can also receive additional support from SCORE.

How to Fund Your Small Business:

The Small Business Administration (SBA.gov) has a microloan program that provides loans of up to $50,000 to be used for start-ups and business growth.[2] Microloans are small loans that are an additional source of loans besides a bank. The average loan amount is $13,000. The borrower can save money and pay back the loan over time.

The funds are provided through an intermediary organization. Contact your local SBA district office for more details.

The benefits of these microloans are: 1) the capital is available in small amounts so you don't have to borrow more than you need; 2) the loan term runs from a few months to a few years with equal monthly payments of principal and interest; and 3) the loans are available for those with lower credit scores. If you have no credit history, you could take out a "credit-builder" loan (a short-term, small loan) to help build up your credit. You must be 18 or 21 years old, depending on the lender. You must be the sole principal or apply with your co-owner. For more information, check out the non-profit economic development organizations that are certified by the Small Business Administration (SBA.gov). These loans are for working capital, money you will use to run your business.

MY BUSINESS IDEA

My product or service is: _____

_____

My customers are (teens, seniors, homeowners, pet owners, etc.): _____

_____

My geographic area to sell is: _____

_____

My competitors are: _____

_____

My business offers: _____ that is different and better than my

competition: _____

_____

What I will need to do to launch my business: _____

_____

_____

My sales strategy is: _____

_____

_____

NOTES:

11

Support Services for Veterans

IF YOU ARE A veteran, your fellow Americans and organizations want to thank you for your service. Don't underestimate yourself. Vets come with a "can do" attitude. They know how to follow orders but they also know how to use their initiative and solve problems.

Over 200,000 servicemen and women transition out of the military every year. There are many organizations to support veterans' needs. One reason that vets are having a hard time when they return home is adjusting to civilian life. A big challenge is to find work and housing to support themselves and their families.

Getting organized is key to the job search. To start, the Department of Veterans Affairs advises that you have copies of your Report of Separation and Verification of Military Experience and Training (DD-214) to verify your military service.[1] Provide transcripts of any military training and coursework that you completed. The Department of Labor (Dol.gov/vets/programs/tap) transition assistance program offers workshops to help with transition.

Helpful Job Sites for Vets:

In the military, jobs are usually assigned. Outside the military, it's a different story. There are workshops given at military bases to help military personnel adapt their skills to a civilian work environment. Part of what is taught is networking. Networking requires knowing how and where to get information for job opportunities. This section will give you a running start. Social media sites like Twitter and LinkedIn can help you make contacts in your job search. Monster.com has a blog (3 ways social media can help vets make the civilian transition). Look at: Indeed.com/military and many others.

Military.com has a military jobs decoder on its website. Veterans can enter a military title or job code and see what the civilian job equivalent would be. Their job search is easier when they change their military accomplishments into civilian language. Many military skills can be used in non-military positions. For example, a pilot demonstrates that he or she is tech-savvy, analytical and can make good decisions quickly. A service man or woman works well under pressure, leads small teams and has good follow-through skills. Every veteran has discipline, the ability to solve problems and work effectively with others. These are transferable skills that can be used in most any job.

Fields that hire more vets include the defense industries, law enforcement and logistics. You need to think about whether you wish to continue working in a similar field to the job you had in the military or change direction and work in a new career. As a veteran, you have a lot to offer. You are adaptable. You had to learn to stay ahead of difficult situations. You have courage. You are resilient. Your strengths will help you to find your way and make a difference at home.

On the website O-Net (Onet.org), go to "my next move for veterans," and it will walk you through the steps giving a lot of information about career options, skills, interests, and what job fields are growing in your area. For example, it lists twenty-three occupations using the skills of a supplies chain officer. You can type in the title of the job you held in the military. It will bring up comparable civilian job titles. It offers career information on the type of work you might be interested in.

Go to CareerOneStop.org to learn where eligible veterans may qualify for federal employment and training funds, provided they meet the eligibility criteria of the program they are applying for. Click on: Veterans Transition Center. It will give you resources for training and jobs. They also have workshops on resume writing, skills assessment and other helpful information.

John applied for a job as manager of a retail store. He was a former army officer. John thought about how his skills could be used on the job he applied for. He listed his experience as troop leader, the manager of a Base PX and his responsibility for inventory control. The interviewer saw a match between his experience in management and inventory control and the needs of the store. He was offered the job.

TIPS TO DO WELL:

When going on an interview, dress in street clothes (no uniform). Use civilian time instead of military time. Translate your military skills into civilian terms before you write your resume and go on an interview. The hiring manager might not understand military terminology. Keep the conversation focused on the skills you can offer for the job you are applying for.

Specific Job Sites For Veterans:

1. DAV.org (Disabled American Veterans) is a nationwide, nonprofit charity that provides employment resources, job fairs and free rides to disabled American veterans.

2. GIJobs.com is a veteran employment center.

3. HelmetsToHardHats.org offers training in the construction industry.

4. HireHerosUSA.org offers career coaching and employment workshops.

5. HirePurpose.com is a job search site.

6. HireVeterans.com helps you find jobs and locate job fairs.

7. Indeed.com/veterans that allows you to enter the title of the job you want and your desired location.

8. Military.com/verteransjobs offers many resources. provides veteran and military spouse resources.

9. Monster.com/hire-veterans is another job board that lets you enter job titles and ideal locations.

10. ResumeEngine.org provides veteran and military spouse recsurces.

11. SimplyHired.com/veterans additionally searches by job tiles and locations

12. VetJobs.com is a job search database and offers resume coaching.

American Corporate Partners (acp-usa.org) is a nonprofit organization that helps veterans in their transition from the armed forces to civilian life. Their Veterans Mentoring Program pairs post-2001 veterans in one-to-one mentoring opportunities. At their online site veterans can post questions regarding job opportunities. HireOurHeroesUSA has partnered with American Corporate Partners to develop a mentoring program to help veterans transition to civilian work. Email their staff for an application: info@acp-usa.org.

TRAINING AND EDUCATION:

There are thousands of post-9/11 veterans attending public and private colleges and accredited trade schools, including culinary arts and auto mechanic training schools. Returning vets must have been activated for a minimum of ninety days after 9/11/2001. They can then qualify for free tuition, fees, books and a monthly allowance when attending a state college or receive up to $18,077 in tuition credits. The post-9/11 GI Bill offers 36 months of educational expenses. These benefits can be transferred to family members, but you need to have served for four more years when you sign up for the benefit. Some states offer their own college funding programs to military families. For a state-by-state list, click on "finding a school" tab on Military.com.

Military spouses are eligible to receive up to $2,000 a year for two years to cover training in healthcare, education, financial services, hospitality management and financial services, as well as training in skilled trades, such as carpentry, electrical work and plumbing. Many colleges offer spouse tuition discounts and also scholarships and grants.

Scholarships For Vets:

Don't overlook military scholarships to help veterans. Local community scholarships from groups like the Rotary Club, the Elks, churches and other civic groups are all less competitive than national scholarships. Check out:

- CareerOneStop.org/findscholarships
- Collegescholarships.org
- MyScholly.com

- Check out Scholarships.com (with information on more than 230,000 schools)

Contact the scholarship resource that you are interested in and send your information to them directly instead of entering it online.

Go to MilitaryTimes.com for a list of the best colleges for veterans. Some states offer funding to military families. Alaska waives 100% of in-state undergraduate tuition for spouses and veterans' dependents. For a state-by-state list, go to Military.com.

Training Assistance:

Many colleges offer online courses and resources on their website for veterans. Military tuition assistance is available from all branches of the service. It covers 100% of in-state tuition. In some community colleges, tuition may be waived for veterans, active duty military and others. Many classes are offered to earn certification in a specific skill or training area.

The Warrior Scholar Project helps veterans transition from the battlefield to the classroom.[2] They teach three things: critical reading, critical writing and adjusting to civilian life. The week-long academic boot camp is taught by veterans. One student said, "They know how to talk to you and put what you've done before in the service to what you can be doing now." To apply, go to WarriorScholar.org.

VFW.org has a pilot program (Veteran Employment Tools) to help people train in automotive maintenance.

Clemente's classes offer a veterans' initiative program. A course directory at their website lists their locations: ClementeCourse.org/about-us/veterans.[3] It focuses on aspects of veteran culture and helps vets work in community service. Courses are free.

Support Services:

In the military, emotion might be seen as a weakness. When veterans comes home, their feelings and demons often stay hidden. Some are embarrassed to say "I need some help." Support group organizations and their mentors give veterans the strength and empowerment they forgot they had. These people and organizations make a difference in helping vets get their lives back.

The HomeBase organization is a good example. HomeBase.org is a national program to support not only the veteran but the entire family.[4] The program recognizes that there is a strong mind-body connection and has developed programs to address veterans' struggles after returning home from active duty.

Sergeant Ryan Pitts, a Medal of Honor recipient, spoke at the HomeBase organization dinner in Boston, Massachusetts on Veteran's Day 2016. He said, "Be easier on yourself. Go get help. The invisible scars of war do not define who you are." The HomeBase organization offers resiliency programs for either a two-week, intensive clinical program or a program that can be taken online. The staff will help you decide which program is right for you. They partner with Massachusetts General Hospital, the Warrior Care Network and it's sponsor, The Boston Red Sox. They developed "The Resilient Warrior" program, designed to reduce the impact of stress through mindfulness and other skill-building exercises. With support, veterans can see beyond their pain and makes plans for their future. They learn that the invisible wounds of war do not define them. They find answers to questions like, "How can I build a better life?" Those changes can be transformative.

Veteran Caregiver Support:

- Legion.org

- HiddenHeroes.org supports military and veteran caregivers.

- Caregiver.va.gov A caregiver peer support mentoring program, pairs veterans with a mentor volunteer for six months.

- USO.org/pathfinder helps service members and their spouses with transition services.

ADDITIONAL HELP FOR FEMALE VETERANS:

Many female veterans come home to no job and a lack of affordable housing. They find it difficult to manage their home life. One woman vet came home but had continuing nightmares. Adjusting to home life was very hard. Through a friend, she heard of Grace After Fire, at GraceAfterFire.org, a nonprofit with locations in San Antonio and Houston, Texas. They run peer support groups. There, she learned how to ask for help when needed. She now gives back by working as an outreach counselor.

Many companies have hired veterans, including CVS, Coca-Cola, Dollar General, Starbucks, Walmart and many more.

Female veterans make up 15% of active duty military force today.[5] In 2017, the Walmart Foundation and Boston University School of Medicine researchers developed a women veterans' network and co-sponsored Veteran's Edge.[5] Their goal is to create a nationwide community for women veterans online (WoVeNWomenVets.org). The pilot program began in August, 2017 in Pittsburgh, Pennsylvania; San Antonio, Texas; and Charlotte, North Carolina. It seeks to benefit female veterans who might feel isolated and helps them adjust and thrive in civilian life. Additional support may be found at the FoundationForWomenWarriors.org.

Housing Resources:

The Fallen Patriot Fund helps families of veterans who were killed or seriously wounded. The family must be in extreme financial hardship. and unemployable as a direct result of disabilities sustained in Operation Iraqi Freedom. Go to their website, FallenPatriotFund.org, to apply for a grant.

FinalSaluteInc.org offers career counseling, financial assistance and childcare for women who are homeless or facing homelessness. Their HOME program is based in the D.C. metro area but has helped women veterans and their families in over thirty states.

Fisherhouse.org offers free or low-cost temporary housing for families of hospitalized military.

Habitat.org is a non-profit organization that helps people build or improve a place they can call home.

HomesForOurTroops.org is a nonprofit that builds specially adapted, mortgage-free homes for veterans that have had severe injuries from their military service.

The HUD-VA.gov Supportive Housing Program offers rental assistance and social services programs.

OperationFinallyHome.org is a nonprofit that offers 100% mortgage-free homes to wounded veterans who qualify.

OperationHomeFront.org (a nationwide program) helps veterans remain in their homes by increasing safety and accessibility.

OperationWeAreHere.com is a clearinghouse of veteran services and opportunity locators for veteran families and supporters.

VeteransInc.org offers housing services and health and wellness outreach and job training.

WeSoldierOn.org is a transitional housing cooperative that provides homeless women veterans with individual plans including financial awareness classes, financial assistance for training and education, and transportation to and from appointments and services. They have locations in Leeds and Pittsfield, Massachusetts.

From Military To Self-Employment:

Only 4.5% of the 3.6 million people who have served in the military since 2001 have started veteran-owned businesses. (Roughly 162,000). There are hurdles that account for that statistic. The G.I. Bill does not provide access to low-interest loans to start a business like the G.I. Bill of World War II did. Women veteran-owned businesses have grown four-fold from 2007 to 2012, according to the U.S. Department of Census.

The Small Business Administration (SBA.gov) has locations across the U.S. Their programs are free and offer information from technical assistance to finding start-up capital. They also offer support for veterans and military spouses, and for National Guard and Reserve members. Refer to Chapter 10 for more information.

There are many more wonderful organizations and businesses dedicated to helping veterans. Please check in your local area to get the support that you deserve. Search support services for vets and companies that are hiring.

Loretta Laroche, a comedian, labeled herself "a humor consultant." Her show, *"Life is not a Stress Rehearsal,"* helps the organization HeroesInTransition.org provide service dogs, home modification and other support as needed.[6] She said that the proceeds from her shows helps those local veterans who have PTSD (post-traumatic stress disorder).

Laroche also said, "If you witness your own absurdities, you will get through life easier. Energy goes with your intentions. If you concentrate on what could go wrong, you will start feeling depressed. By visualizing positive joy and envisioning things going right, you can help transform your life and make a difference in the lives of others."

Her organization also trains service dogs to help veterans adjust to civilian life. Another organization that provides that same support for veterans is Hero-Dogs.org.

"LIGHT-HEARTED HUMOR IS THE KEY TO THE SOUL'S PRESERVATION."

- Loretta LaRoche

SUPPORT SERVICES FOR VETERANS

My needs are: _____

_____

I will contact these places for assistance with: _____

_____

My questions about their services are: _____

_____

My appointment is: _____

I need to bring: _____

_____

_____

NOTES:

12

PROOF OF PROGRESS

IN THESE CHAPTERS, WE DISCUSSED the process of getting into a field that you enjoy, overcoming challenges along the way, and feeling more comfortable and happy within yourself.

You have been learning practical techniques and skills to deal with life's challenges. The power of choice is in your hands. Be aware of your goals and priorities. It gives you a path to follow in making decisions for your personal life and on the job. There is a process that you can use when things don't go as planned. This process is called resilience.

Resilience means mental toughness. It is a tool to help you through tough times.

Resilience is a learned skill. You are not born with it.

Your coping skills help to develop your resilience.

HOW TO LEARN RESILIENCE:

Develop realistic plans that you can follow through with. Manage your feelings and thoughts. When stressed, get some exercise and talk to someone who is thoughtful and caring. It is important to have positive people on your side.

Resilient people believe that they have the ability to deal with their problems. They use mindfulness to stay more thoughtful and focused. They trust themselves to come up with possible solutions. They stay flexible if things don't work out exactly as planned.

One of the main points of resilience is your perception of a problem as a minor thing or more. If it's not a threat to you, deal with it and move on. See it as a challenge and learn from it. When you believe you are better, you will continue to take the steps to keep on going.

Researchers Dr. Steven Southwick and Dr. Dennis Charney studied resilience.[1] They emphasize the importance of finding resilience-building skills to use when things get tough. Their expert tips[2] are to:

- Develop a strong core set of beliefs that nothing can shake.

- Find meaning in whatever stressful event happens.

- Try to keep a positive outlook.

- Take cues from your mentor or someone who is especially resilient.

- Don't run from what scares you. Face up to what you are afraid of.

- Be quick to reach out and ask for support as soon as you feel that you need it.

- Keep learning. Learn a new thing as often as you can.

- Stick with an exercise program.

- Focus on the present and on your goals.

- Be aware of what makes you strong and own it.

Resilience And Emotional Intelligence:

Resilience and emotional intelligence go hand in hand. They work together to help you be more aware of your positive emotions. You become more motivated and ready when opportunities come along. Learning to make good decisions gives you the strength to keep moving forward. If your first try didn't work out, think of another plan. Look at a setback as a signal, not a roadblock. Ask what you can do to find another way to reach your goal. With your new-found resilience, attitude and practice, you can do more than just an acceptable job. Your positive attitude will build your optimism.

Optimism, one key to your success, can be learned:

Optimism:

Your **talents**, your **motivation** and the **belief** that you can do it are all part of optimism. Optimism is a learned skill. It is learning how to look at a negative thought in a more positive way. It plays a huge part in being successful at what you do.

Dr. Martin Seligman, a noted psychologist, said that "those who learned optimism do better in all parts of their lives: relationships, work, family, school and sports.[3] The good news is that when a person is taught that his or her actions make a difference, those feelings of helplessness get smaller. There will always be obstacles, but you will learn how to manage them."

Dr. Seligman continues: "Optimism is not the same as being unrealistic. It is realizing the facts. It is remembering the good experiences in your life. That gives you the strength to carry on. If your mood is down, use optimism. If you are applying for a job, use optimism. If your goal is risky behavior, do not use optimism."

Look around. When you change how you look at things, you can change your focus. You are giving yourself another chance at reaching your goals. Your confidence is earned through hard work and a clearer understanding of what you have to offer. There is a strong connection between your emotions and the career you are striving for.

Tom Chappell, who started the Tom's of Maine company said, "An optimist is not necessarily someone who looks on the bright side of things, but someone who understands practical ways to make things happen."[4]

Take advantage of any training or education that will help in your chosen field. Reach out and connect with people who can assist you along the way. You might motivate them to go for a better career too. Take all this information as your tools to do well. Invest in yourself.

Persistence Pays:

Your goals change as you move forward. Continue to make new goals to stay on track. You are building a toolbox of skills to use when the unexpected happens. You are working toward a better job for you and your family. Live life in the present but always keep your eye to the future. Show courage. Realize that *you* are the change you are looking for. Get some help from your mentor and others.

Mike Krzyewski, the coach of the men's basketball team at Duke University, said, "Give yourself the gift of success. You need to merge your preparedness with the passion to win. When you do that, there's a good chance that you're going to succeed."[5]

LOOKING AHEAD:

Remember when you started this journey? The motivating tools and strategies, the steps you've so carefully taken, will help you achieve more than you thought was possible. The information learned will help you for a long time going forward. This is a lifelong approach, not a quick fix. Motivate yourself. Then, be a mentor to others.

> "IF YOU CANT FLY, THEN RUN.
>
> IF YOU CAN'T RUN, THEN WALK.
>
> IF YOU CAN'T WALK, THEN CRAWL.
>
> BUT WHATEVER YOU DO, YOU HAVE TO
> KEEP MOVING FORWARD."
>
> -Martin Luther King, Jr.

MY JOURNEY SO FAR

It is the beginning of my new life.

I am proud. My accomplishments are_____

_____

_____

What I learned about myself is_____

_____

An example of how I showed my resilience: _____

_____

I used my optimism when_____

_____

I will use what I learned to _____

_____

I will help others to_____

_____

NOTES:

REFERENCES:

NOTE: the page numbers below refer to pages within this guide.

Chapter 1: Change Starts Here

p.3. (1) *Shame and Guilt*, June Price Tangney, Rhonda L. Dearing, The Guilford Press, New York, 2013

p.3. (2) "Social Relationships and Mortality Risk," Julianne Holt-Lundstat, Health.com, September, 2015

p.4. (3) "Life is Like a Kaleidoscope," a story about bullying, Evelyn Jackson, *Cape Cod Times*, June 20, 2013

p.4. (4) "Henry Winkler's Story," *Parade Magazine*, August 21, 2016

p.5. (5) "When we are no longer able to change a situation, we are challenged to change ourselves," quote by Viktor Frankl, author of *Man's Search for Meaning*, Beacon Press, 2006

p.5. (6) "Moving Forward requires Positive Thinking," Judith Sills, *Psychology Today*: Let-It-Go, November, 2014

p.6. (7) David Ortiz, Commencement Speech, *ABC News*, April 30, 2017

Chapter 2: Ways To Cope

p.10. (1) *Thoughts and Feelings*, Matthew McKay, Martha David, and Patrick Fanning, New Harbinger Publishing Company, Thousand Oaks, CA, 2007

p.11. (2) "Single Mom, Single Mission," *Savannah Morning News*, January, 2016

p.14. (3) *The Lost Art of Listening*, Michael P. Nichols, Guilford Press, New York, New York, 2009

p.15. (4) *Self-Compassion,* Dr. Kristin Neff, William Morrow Publishing, New York, 2011

Chapter 3: Be Mindful

p.19. (1) "Mindfulness," coined by Jon Kabat-Zinn, Director of the Stress Reduction Clinic, University of Massachusetts Medical School, Amherst, MA.

p.19. (2) "Mindfulness Produces Less-Stressed Marines," Dr. Martin Paulus and Elizabeth Stanley, *Pacific Standard* newspaper article, May 16, 2014

p.20. (3) "Eight-Weeks to a Better Brain," a program of Mindfulness and Stress Reduction, Dr. Sara Lazar, *Harvard Gazette,* Harvard Medical School, Cambridge, MA, January 21, 2011

p.20. (4) *10% Happier*, Dan Harris, Harper-Collins Books, New York, 2014

p.22. (5) *Oneness with All Life*, Eckhart Tolle, Dutton Publishing, New York, 2008

p.22. (6) "Happiness Tips," *The Boston Globe*, Boston, MA, March 10, 2006

Chapter 4: The Value Of A Mentor

p.25. (1) "Chaplain Dave," Sara Hoagland, *PrimeTime Magazine,* December 20, 2003

p.26. (2) "Mentoring that Works," K. C. Meyers, capecodonline.com, April 22, 2015

p.26. (3) "Washing Dishes from Jeff," *Readers' Digest*, April, 2016

Chapter 5: You Have Potential

p.33. (1) "The Story of George," by Joan Graham, *Prime Time Magazine,* June, 2015

p.35. (2) *Smarter, Faster, Better,* Charles Duhigg, Random House, New York, 2017

p.35. (3) *Mindset, The New Psychology of Success,* Carol S. Dweck, Ballantine Books, New York, 2007

p.36. (4) "Woman goes from Homeless to Harvard," *WCVB Boston*, May 18, 2017

Chapter 6: The Power Of Choice

p.40. (1) "Sheer Force of Will," the story of Sean, *Cape Cod Times*, Steven Withrow, August 25, 2017 p.41. (2) *Do What You Are,* Paul Tieger and Barbara Baron Tieger, Little Brown and Company, New York, 1992

p.41. (3) *Discover What You're Best At*, Linda Gale and Barry Gale, A Fireside Book Publication, Simon and Schuster, New York, 1998

Chapter 7: Work-Related Training And Education

p.54. (1) The story of Eddie "The Reluctant Learner," *The Salem Statement*, Salem University, Salem, Massachusetts, Winter, 2016

p.56. (2) "Job-Training-Can-Work-So-Why-Isn't-There-More-Of-It," www.nytimes.com/business/economy/, Eduardo Porter, July 5, 2016

p.58. (3) "High School Equivalency Graduates Lauded," capecodonline.com, June 2, 2016

p.59. (4) "Tech Firms Train Their Own Workers," Associated Press, by Emory Dalesio, November 24, 2017

p.59. (5) CiviCorps, Associated Press, November 25, 2016

p.60. (6) "When Expert Tradespeople are Hard to Find," *The Washington Post*, by Brenda Richardson, April 19, 2018

p.64. (7) "The Art of the Deal," Clemente Courses, *The Washington Post Magazine*, June 2, 2017

p.65. (8) "Regina's Story," *Inspire Health Magazine*, June, 2016

Chapter 8: Dealing With Obstacles

p.70. (1) *Working With Emotional Intelligence,* Daniel Goleman, Bantam Books, New York, January, 2000

p.72. (2) *The Champion's Comeback*," Jim Afremow, Rodale Books, New York, 2010

Chapter Nine: Job Search Strategies

pp.91-92. (1) "The Jobs Program," Michigan Prevention Research Center for Job Search Training, Robert Caplan and Richard Price, 1984-2000

Chapter 10: Starting A Small Business

p.107. (1) "Just a Good Idea Might Work," *Cape Cod Times*, March 25, 2015

p. 107. (2) "Twenty-Five Characteristics of Success," James Stephenson, *Entrepreneur Magazine*, March 12, 2014

p.108. (3) "Recipe for Success," Paul Romano, *Fortune Magazine*, March 28, 2015

Chapter 11: Veteran Support Services

p.113. (1) Department of Labor (DOL.gov) Transition Assistance programs

p.117. (2) "Warrior Scholar Project Helps Veterans Transition From Battlefield To Classroom," CBSNEWS, August 15, 2017

p.113. (3) Clementecourse.org/about-us/veterans

pp.117-118. (4) HomeBase.org, WCVB-TV, November 13, 2015

p.119. (5) "Easing the Transition to Civilian Life for Women Veterans," *Bostonia Magazine*, Summer, 2017

pp.120-121 (6) "Help Veterans with Humor," Loretta LaRoche, *Cape Cod Times*, April 22, 2016

Chapter 12: Proof Of Progress

p.126. (1) *Resilience: The Science of Mastering Life's Greatest Challenges*, Dr. Steven Southwick, Cambridge University Press, Cambridge, England, 2012

p.126. (2) "Expert tips for Resilience," Dr. Dennis Charney and Dr. Steven Southwick, *Time Magazine*, June 1, 2015

p.127. (3) *Learned Optimism*, Martin E. Seligman, Alfred A. Knopf , New York, 1990

p.127. (4) "The-Very-Long-Road," Tom Chappell, founder of Tom's of Maine Toothpaste, *INC Magazine*," July 1, 2017

p.128. (5) "Life's Work: An interview with Mike Krzyewski," *Harvard Business Review* (HBR.org), March, 2017

FIND IT HERE (A KEY WORD INDEX)

D

E

F

G

H

I

J

K

INDEX OF HELPFUL WEBSITES

5. High School Equivalency Test (GED in some states):

Your state's Board of Education will also have a website.

6. Online Courses:

7. Online Job Search:

There are many more job search sites. These are some of the largest. Search by job title and location.

8. Professional Support:

9. Salary Information:

10. Scholarships:

11. Training Resources:

12. Veterans Services:

13. Job Training:

14. Support Services:

15. Additional Help For Female Veterans:

16. Housing Resources:

There are many more organizations than can be listed here. Please search for the support you deserve. Check out: Support Services for veterans and companies that are hiring veterans.

ABOUT THE AUTHOR

Author Diane Singer has helped hundreds of people, young and old, find the career they wanted. As an experienced recruiter, job coach, counselor and mentor, she knows what employers are looking for and the steps you need to take to get the job you want.

She offers expertise in career counseling and employee recruitment, stemming in part from more than a decade as a member of the Boston University Alumni Career Network. A consultant to management in a wide range of industries, Singer has extensive experience working with all levels of recruitment and staffing.

She has developed and implemented training programs on interviewing, resume writing, career transitioning and skills development. Singer has been a frequent guest speaker at One Stop Career Shops in Massachusetts, for nonprofit organizations and on military bases.

Professional affiliations include: College Alumni Career Counselor, Boston University; Northeast Counselors' Association; American Personnel and Guidance Association; Northeast Human Resources Association; and the National Association of Personnel Services, where she has served on the National Board of Directors.

She holds an M.Ed. in Counseling Psychology from Salem University and a B.A. in Psychology from Boston University, as well as Human Resource Management education from Babson College.

Made in the
USA
Middletown, DE